Brian Fleming Research & Learning Library
Ministry of Education
Ministry of Training, Colleges & Universities
900 Bay St. 13th Floor, Mowat Block
Toronto, ON M7A 1L2

Improving Student Achievement:
50 More Research-Based Strategies for Educators

Beverly Nichols, PhD

Professional Development Resources for K–12
Library Media and Technology Specialists

Rather than putting a trademark symbol at every occurrence of a trademarked name, we state that we are using the names in an editorial manner only and to the benefit of the trademark owner, with no intention of infringement of the trademark.

Library of Congress Cataloging-in-Publication Data

Nichols, Beverly (Beverly W.)
  Improving student achievement : 50 more research-based strategies for educators / Beverly Nichols.
      p. cm.
  Includes bibliographical references and index.
  ISBN-13: 978-1-58683-290-2 (pbk.)
  ISBN-10: 1-58683-290-5 (pbk.)
  1. Academic achievement--United States. 2. School improvement programs--United States. 3. Teacher effectiveness--United States. 4. Learning strategies--United States. I. Title.
  LB1062.6.N54 2009
  371.2'07--dc22
                          2008052905

Cynthia Anderson: Editor
Judi Repman: Consulting Editor

Published by Linworth Publishing, Inc.
3650 Olentangy River Road
Suite 250
Columbus, Ohio 43214

Copyright © 2009 by Linworth Publishing, Inc.

All rights reserved. Purchasing this book entitles a librarian to reproduce activity sheets for use in the library within a school or entitles a teacher to reproduce activity sheets for single classroom use within a school. Other portions of the book (up to 15 pages) may be copied for staff development purposes within a single school. Standard citation information should appear on each page. The reproduction of any part of this book for an entire school or school system or for commercial use is strictly prohibited. No part of this book may be electronically reproduced, transmitted, or recorded without written permission from the publisher.

ISBN 13: 978-1-58683-290-2
ISBN 10: 1-58683-290-5

5 4 3 2 1

Table of Contents

Sample PowerPoint Presentation vi

About the Author x

Introduction xi

Section I: Leadership 1
- Research Tip #1: School Boards and Student Achievement 2
- Research Tip #2: Instructional Leadership at the District Level 4
- Research Tip #3: Instructional Leadership by Principals 6
- Research Tip #4: Teachers as Leaders 8
- Research Tip #5: Effective Staff Meetings 10
- Research Tip #6: Staff Meetings as Professional Development 12
- Research Tip #7: Time Management Tips for Principals 14

Section II: Meeting the Needs of All Children 17
- Research Tip #8: Differentiation 18
- Research Tip #9: Autism 20
- Research Tip #10: Dyslexia 22
- Research Tip #11: ADD-ADHD 24
- Research Tip #12: Success with Hispanic Students 26
- Research Tip #13: Response to Intervention 28
- Research Tip #14: Preschool and Early Childhood 30
- Research Tip #15: The Gender Gap and Single-Sex Education 32

Section III: School Structure and Organization 35
- Research Tip #16: Year-Round Schools 36
- Research Tip #17: Impact of Block Scheduling 38
- Research Tip #18: Grade Level Configuration 40
- Research Tip #19: School Size and Small Learning Communities 42
- Research Tip #20: Looping 44

Section IV: Intervention Programs 47
- Research Tip #21: Grade Retention and Social Promotion 48
- Research Tip #22: The Summer Slide 50
- Research Tip #23: Effective Summer Programs 52
- Research Tip #24: Effective After-School Programs 54

Section V: Technology 57
- Research Tip #25: Status and Challenges of Technology 58
- Research Tip #26: Technology's Impact on Achievement 60
- Research Tip #27: Virtual Learning 62

Section VI: Brain-Based Learning 65
- Research Tip #28: The Brain and Attention 66
- Research Tip #29: The Brain and Memory 68
- Research Tip #30: More Strategies for Brain-Based Learning 70

Section VII: Advanced Placement 73
- Research Tip #31: Advanced Placement and Student Achievement 74
- Research Tip #32: Challenges of Advanced Placement Implementation 76

Section VIII: Special Certification Status 79
- Research Tip #33: The Impact of Alternative Certification 80
- Research Tip #34: Board-Certified Teachers and Student Achievement 82

Section IX: Health Issues 85
- Research Tip #35: Obesity and Physical Education 86
- Research Tip #36: Schools and Nutrition 88

Section X: Language and Literacy 91
- Research Tip #37: International Language at the Elementary Level 92
- Research Tip #38: International Language at the Secondary Level 94
- Research Tip #39: The Status of Writing 96
- Research Tip #40: Effective Writing Instruction 98
- Research Tip #41: Writing across the Curriculum 100
- Research Tip #42: Sustained Silent Reading 102
- Research Tip #43: Reading Aloud: Teachers and Parents 104
- Research Tip #44: Libraries and Learning 106

Section XI: Social Studies 109
- Research Tip #45: The Status of Social Studies 110
- Research Tip #46: Effective Instruction in Social Studies 112
- Research Tip #47: Service Learning 114

Section XII: Classroom Management, Discipline, and Safety Issues 117
- Research Tip #48: Cyber Bullies 118
- Research Tip #49: Proactive Classroom Management 120
- Research Tip #50: Dealing with Disruptive Behavior 122

Resources 124

Index 131

CD Table of Contents

PowerPoint® Presentations

Research Tip #1	School Boards and Student Achievement
Research Tip #2	Instructional Leadership at the District Level
Research Tip #3	Instructional Leadership by Principals
Research Tip #4	Teachers as Leaders
Research Tip #5	Effective Staff Meetings
Research Tip #6	Staff Meetings as Professional Development
Research Tip #7	Time Management Tips for Principals
Research Tip #8	Differentiation
Research Tip #9	Autism
Research Tip #10	Dyslexia
Research Tip #11	ADD-ADHD
Research Tip #12	Success with Hispanic Students
Research Tip #13	Response to Intervention
Research Tip #14	Preschool and Early Childhood
Research Tip #15	The Gender Gap and Single-Sex Education
Research Tip #16	Year-Round Schools
Research Tip #17	Impact of Block Scheduling
Research Tip #18	Grade Level Configuration
Research Tip #19	School Size and Small Learning Communities
Research Tip #20	Looping
Research Tip #21	Grade Retention and Social Promotion
Research Tips #22-23	The Summer Slide and Effective Summer Programs
Research Tip #24	Effective After-School Programs
Research Tips #25-26	The Status and Impact of Technology
Research Tip #27	Virtual Learning
Research Tip #28	The Brain and Attention
Research Tip #29	The Brain and Memory
Research Tip #30	More Strategies for Brain-Based Learning
Research Tips #31-32	Advanced Placement—Status and Challenges
Research Tip #33	The Impact of Alternative Certification
Research Tip #34	Board-Certified Teachers and Student Achievement
Research Tips #35-36	Obesity, Nutrition, and Physical Education
Research Tip #37	International Language at the Elementary Level
Research Tip #38	International Language at the Secondary Level
Research Tips #39-40	Writing Instruction
Research Tip #41	Writing across the Curriculum
Research Tips #42-43	Sustained Silent Reading and Reading Aloud
Research Tip #44	Libraries and Learning
Research Tips #45-46	Social Studies
Research Tip #47	Service Learning
Research Tip #48	Cyber Bullies
Research Tips #49-50	Classroom Management

Note: the tips above are listed in numerical order. It should be noted, however, that on the CD containing the PowerPoint presentations the list of files appears in a slightly different order. All the singletons are listed first, followed by those presentations that consist of two or more combined tips.

The following is a sample of one of the PowerPoint presentations included on the CD.

Sustained Silent Reading and Reading Aloud
Research Tips 42 and 43

Sustained Silent Reading

The issue:
Researchers in the field of reading consistently report that the more students read, the more competent they become as readers. In 1985 the Commission on Reading, in its report *Becoming a Nation of Readers*, recommended two hours a week of independent reading.

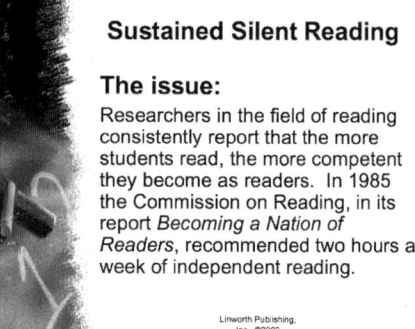

The issue:
Commission members recommended that time for this could be found by eliminating some of the time spent on skill sheets and workbooks. Proponents of sustained silent reading (SSR) used this recommendation to support expansion of SSR programs.

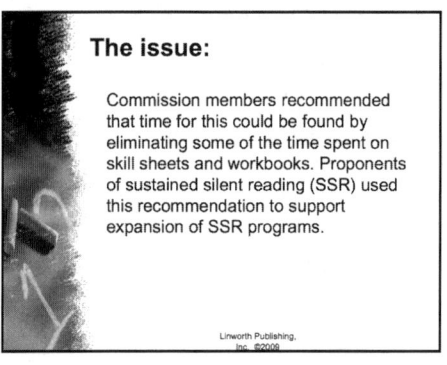

The issue:
Yet in 2000 the National Reading Panel report stated there wasn't sufficient scientific evidence to support the use of SSR in schools. These disparate positions lead to the question, "What does the research tell us?"

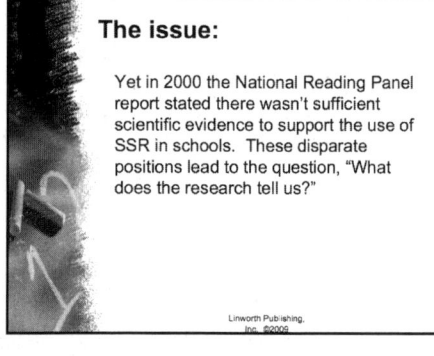

The research:
- Krashen describes three types of free voluntary reading:
  - sustained silent reading (SSR), in which both teachers and students participate in independent reading for a set amount of time each day or week;
  - self-selected reading, in which teachers hold conferences with students to discuss what the students have read; and
  - extensive reading, which has minimal accountability on the student's part.

The research:
- While some research has addressed the broader picture of free voluntary reading, sustained silent reading (SSR) has received specific attention in many studies.
- The typical elementary school class spends less than 10% of its total reading instruction on independent silent reading.

The research:

- Surveys of elementary teachers indicate that fewer than half their schools incorporate SSR as standard operating procedure.
- Research has repeatedly shown a correlation between the amount of time spent reading and overall reading achievement, including vocabulary and fluency.

The research:

- Research on in-school free reading programs indicates that such programs also have a positive impact on grammar and writing.
- An analysis of 54 studies that compared schools with planned free voluntary reading to schools without such a program found that students in schools with the programs consistently did as well or better than students without such a program.

The research:

- Positive effects were found in 25 of the studies, with duration of the program having a direct impact on student achievement results.
- One study that found little difference in overall achievement found that statistically significant differences were apparent when students interacted with one another to discuss what they had read.

The research:

- Studies have found that students who participate in planned free-reading programs (such as SSR) do more independent, voluntary reading than students who do not participate in such programs.
- One study that included a follow-up of adolescent boys found that the students who had participated in an extended free reading program were reading more six years later than students who had not participated in such a program.

The research:

- Studies that have analyzed how students actually use their time during sustained silent reading (SSR) have found that 90 percent or more of the students were involved in reading.
- The involvement was highest when books from which students could choose were provided in the classroom, when teachers actively promoted some books, and when the teachers themselves were involved in reading during SSR.

The research:

- International studies comparing the reading skills of children in over thirty countries found two consistent factors among those with the highest reading scores: they were students who were read to daily by their teachers and who read the most pages independently for pleasure.

Practical implications:

- SSR programs that have contributed to improved reading skills in participating students have common attributes.
- The program is of sufficient duration to make an impact. Those programs that lasted six months or more had the greatest effect. Researchers indicate it may take four to five months to get students engaged in the process.
- The environment for SSR is conducive to quiet, uninterrupted reading.

Practical implications:

- A wide variety of materials is available, addressing both interest levels and readability. Students are allowed to choose what they want to read unless a selection is totally inappropriate.
- Teachers and other staff members serve as role models. All adults read during the SSR time. Teachers are enthusiastic about their reading and encourage reading for pleasure on the part of their students.

Questions to ask ourselves:

- What steps do we need to take to implement an SSR program in our school?
- Are staff members supportive of such a program?
- Do we have the variety of reading materials we need to launch such a program?
- How would we evaluate the effectiveness of the program?

Questions to ask ourselves:

- If we already have an SSR program do we know if it is achieving the desired results?
- How can we determine the answer to that question?

Reading Aloud

The issue:

"The single most important activity for building the knowledge required for eventual success in reading is reading aloud to children."

The issue:

This research-based conclusion from the 1985 report of the Commission on Reading has been a catalyst for increased attention to a practice that was coming into its own as an instructional strategy a quarter of a century ago. What does more recent research tell us about the prevalence of the practice and its impact as a teaching and learning tool?

The research:

- The prevalence of reading aloud has increased dramatically over time. The proportion of elementary teachers who reported they read aloud to their students before 1985 was less than half.
- A study completed in 2000 indicated that 100% of elementary teachers reported that they read aloud to their students on a regular basis.

The research:

- At middle school, where the reported incidence of teachers reading aloud to students is much lower, students themselves report that listening to their teachers read aloud is a favorite literacy activity.

The research:

- Jim Trelease, in *The Read-Aloud Handbook*, cites specific benefits for reading aloud.
  - Reading aloud creates background knowledge.
  - Reading aloud builds vocabulary.
  - Reading aloud provides a reading role model.

The research:

- Reading aloud conditions a child's brain to associate reading with pleasure.
  - Identifying reading as an activity or experience that brings pleasure contributes to increased reading.
  - Increased reading, in turn, leads to more highly developed reading skills.

viii / *Improving Student Achievement: 50 More Research-Based Strategies for Educators*

The research:

A summary of research from Stephen Krashen related to the benefits of reading aloud includes the following findings.

The research:

- The positive impact of reading aloud to children begins with experiences in the home and at the preschool level.
- Several studies indicate that children read more independently when they have been read to at home. In such cases, parents appear to have established routines for reading to their children starting at an early age.

The research:

- Classroom teachers may not be able to influence what happens at home or in preschool experiences, but they can use reading aloud in their classrooms to produce positive results.
- Children who are read to regularly whether at home or school make large gains in both vocabulary and reading comprehension when compared to children who are not read to on a regular basis.

The research:

- Children's vocabulary knowledge grows as a result of hearing stories with unfamiliar words. Words need to be heard more than once, with discussion of the meaning of individual words.
- Studies indicate that children like being read to. Specific time set aside in the school day for reading aloud has been found to be a motivational factor for students to complete other tasks.

The research:

- Students are more likely to select books for independent reading that have already been read to them than ones with which they are not familiar.

The research:

- A study in a remedial reading class at the college level found that even college level students enjoyed and benefited from being read to by the teacher.
- Benefits were measured by the number of books checked out for independent reading and results on a final essay; comparisons were made between classes in which students were read to and those in which they were not.

Practical implications:

- Hearing a teacher read a story enhances children's comprehension.
- However, just listening is not sufficient.
- Children need to participate in discussion to understand unfamiliar words and to make predictions and inferences about the story.

Practical implications:

- A study of second grade students found that students benefited more from listening to a story being read when they only listened, rather than being asked to listen while following the story in print.
- Observations by researchers indicated that students were not as focused when given the written material to follow.

Questions to ask ourselves:

- What proactive measures have we taken to encourage and support parents of preschoolers in establishing read-aloud practices at home?
- Have we established consistent practices in our school for reading aloud to students, with appropriate time for interaction with students and attention to vocabulary development and comprehension?

Resources:

- Anderson, Richard, Elfrieda Hiebert, Judith Scott, and Ian Wilkinson. *Becoming a Nation of Readers: The Report of the Commission on Reading.* Washington, DC: The National Institute of Education,1985.
- Binkley, Marilyn. "Becoming a Nation of Readers: What Principals Can Do." 1969. 8 July 2008 http://eric.ed.gov/ERICDocs/data/ericdocs2sql/content_storage_01/0000019b/80/1e/35/ce.pdf
- Kaplan, Julie, and Diane Tracey. "Teacher Read-Alouds at 2nd Grade, With and Without Student Companion Texts: Unexpected Findings." 2007. 9 July 2008 <http://eric.ed.gov/ERICDocs/data/ericdocs2sql/content_storage_01/0000019b/80/3d/e0/8a.pdf>.

Resources:

- Krashen, Stephen. *The Power of Reading: Insights from the Research.* Portsmouth, NH: Heinemann, 2004.
- Trelease, Jim. "Chapter 1: Why Read Aloud?" *The Read-Aloud Handbook.* 2001. 8 July 2008 <http//:www.trelease-on-reading.com/rah_chpt1_p2.html>.
- Trelease, Jim. "Chapter 5: Sustained Silent Reading—Reading Aloud's Natural Partner." *The Read-Aloud Handbook.* 2001. 8 July 2008 <http//:www.trelease-on-reading.com/rah_chpt5_p1.html>.

About the Author

Beverly Nichols, PhD

Beverly Nichols is an independent education consultant assisting schools and school systems in many areas of school improvement. She has more than 40 years of experience in mathematics education and educational leadership at both the campus and the district level. Her classroom teaching experience has included elementary and high school classes as well as college level courses in computer programming and mathematics education. Dr. Nichols received her BA and MA from Arizona State University, an Ed.S. in Educational Administration from Emporia State University, and a PhD in curriculum and instruction from the University of Missouri at Kansas City. Dr. Nichols has worked with school districts and individual schools across the United States, assisting them with curriculum and assessment development, interpretation and use of data, and development and implementation of school improvement plans. Her emphasis has been on capacity building for staff members, with attention to knowledge of "what works." She is author of *Improving Student Achievement: 50 Research-Based Strategies* as well as a co-author of *Managing Curriculum and Assessment: A Practitioner's Guide*, both Linworth publications.

Introduction

"Is it research based?" While this question has been asked for a number of years in relation to practices and interventions, the question has become a mantra for educators since the passage and implementation of No Child Left Behind legislation. In the legislation, "scientifically-based research" is the type of research required to justify expenditures of federal money on materials and programs. The focus for scientifically-based research is randomized field trials with control and experimental groups—a type of research difficult to implement with fairness in many educational settings.

This book is the second of two books intended as a resource for busy educators who need a starting point in seeking out evidence related to research-based practices. This book is not intended to include only the type of research prescribed by No Child Left Behind. The information included in the research tips has been gleaned from a variety of sources—meta-analyses and extensive literature reviews as well as standalone studies. Most references included are Web resources to allow for ease of access. The references included in the Web resources may take readers to periodicals and books for additional information. Some references, while more than a decade old, remain as some of the best comprehensive studies available.

Each Research Tip in this book focuses on a topic that is of concern to practicing educators, whether they are classroom teachers, building administrators, or central office administrators. Some tips will be of more interest to specific groups or instructional levels, while other tips will speak to all professionals in the field of public education. The information contained in each tip is by no means all-inclusive; it is meant to provide the reader with a synopsis of information that can be used as:

- a basis for decision making (including expenditure of federal funds);
- the starting point for additional information gathering; or
- as a springboard for professional discussion.

The PowerPoint presentations on the CD that accompany this book contain basically the same information that is found in the text. These presentations can be used as the basis of those professional discussions previously mentioned:

- in school-based faculty meetings;
- in administrative or departmental meetings at the district level; or
- (when appropriate) in meetings with parents.

While each of the 50 tips can stand alone, they are organized so that similar topics are together and can be located easily. This will allow users of the book to access with greater ease those topics of greatest interest to them personally.

Section I: Leadership

RESEARCH TIP #1
School Boards and Student Achievement

The issue:
Strong leadership at the individual school level has long been associated with effective schools whose students demonstrate high achievement. Research findings indicate that district leadership also has an impact on the quality of student learning. But leadership for school districts ultimately starts with the board of education. What does research tell us about boards of education and their impact on student achievement?

> In the high-achieving districts, board members and the superintendent had high expectations for all students, while in the low-achieving districts these leaders believed that factors beyond their control limited students.

The research:
Relatively little empirical research has been conducted to study the relationship between school boards and student achievement. A good deal of available literature focuses on policies and opinion. However, small-scale studies that are available do provide direction.

A study conducted in the late 1990s by the Iowa Association of School Boards is one widely reported study. The study compared the actions of school boards in three consistently high-achieving Iowa districts with the actions of boards in districts with consistently low student achievement. The school districts compared were similar in enrollment, demographic factors, and per pupil spending. In addition, the school boards of all six districts were similar in several ways, including the following:
- They all wanted to do the right thing for children.
- Board members and the superintendent got along with one another, and board members were satisfied with the superintendent.
- None of the districts had been successful in closing the gap between general education children and children with special needs.

Differences in the boards included the following:
- In the high-achieving districts, board members and the superintendent had high expectations for all students, while in the low-achieving districts these leaders believed that factors beyond their control limited students.
- In the high-achieving districts, board members were knowledgeable about major initiatives including curriculum, instruction, assessment and staff development, and could describe the board's role in supporting those initiatives. In the low-achieving districts, board members had limited knowledge of school improvement goals and could not describe actions taking place to meet those goals.
- In the high-achieving district, board members were openly supportive of the staff and encouraged ongoing staff development to enable teachers to better meet students' needs. In the low-achieving district, board members were often critical of teachers and principals and questioned the value of staff development.

A study of four Texas school districts, diverse in population but demonstrating high achievement, identified the role the boards played in student achievement:
- The boards established goals that reflected the belief that all students could learn challenging academic content.

- The boards monitored progress toward those goals but left the management role to the superintendent and the superintendent's staff.

Practical implications:
Iowa school board presidents in successful districts identified common practices that kept board meetings focused on academic achievement:
- Regularly scheduled presentations by departments or individual schools to inform board members of particular programs or specific academic achievement.
- Specific efforts to increase board members' knowledge about issues related to teaching and learning.

The National School Boards Association has emphasized the importance of alignment, with policies that ensure consistency between goals, academic standards, resources, staff development, and assessment.

Goodman and Zimmerman make the following recommendations for school boards:
- Work as a team with the superintendent to create a vision for what education in the district should do for the children being served.
- Develop a management system that will allow the vision to become reality; then provide the superintendent and his or her staff with the resources necessary to implement that system.
- Take time to attend appropriate workshops and conferences to attain appropriate knowledge as well as to learn the leadership skills necessary to be an effective board member.
- Establish procedures to hire the most highly qualified teachers possible, and maintain open and honest communication with the teachers within the district.

Questions to ask ourselves:
- Do we as a school board have a vision for what education in our district looks like?
- Do we have high expectations for all of our students?
- Are we providing our staff with the support and resources needed to attain this vision?

Resources:
Goodman, Richard, and William Zimmerman. "Thinking Differently: Recommendations for 21st Century School Board/Superintendent Leadership, Governance, and Teamwork for High Student Achievement." 2000. 15 Mar. 2009 <http://www.nesdec.org/research_dev/ThinkingDifferently.mht>.
Iowa Association of School Boards. "School Boards and Student Achievement." 2000. 24 Mar. 2008 <http://www.baraboo.k12.wi.us/schoolboard/compass_article.pdf>.
Lashway, Larry. "Using School Board Policy to Improve Student Achievement." *ERIC Digest*. Undated. 24 Mar. 2008 <http://www.ericdigests.org/2003-4/school-board.html>.
National School Boards Association. "Key Work of School Boards." Undated. 15 Mar. 2009 <http://www.nsba.org/MainMenu/Governance/KeyWork/Resources/TrainingMaterials.aspx>.
Porch, Stephanie, and Nancy Protheroe. *School Board-Superintendent Relations in Support of High Student Achievement*. The Informed Educator Series. Alexandria, VA: Educational Research Services, 2006.
Protheroe, Nancy. *School Boards Focused on Student Learning*. The Informed Educator Series. Alexandria, VA: Educational Research Services, 2003.

RESEARCH TIP #2
Instructional Leadership at the District Level

The issue:
In an introduction to the *Education Week* supplement, "Leading for Learning," author Jeff Archer asked a significant question. "What strategies should district leaders pursue to influence the quality of teaching and learning?" Research dealing with the influence of superintendents and other district-level personnel on student learning is limited, and where it exists it is correlational rather than cause-and-effect. However, the evidence that is available provides direction for district administrators who seek to be effective leaders, especially in improving teaching and learning.

> A growing body of evidence indicates that effective schools are most frequently found in school districts that provide strong, system-wide support and guidance.

The research:
Many adjectives are attached to types of leadership—instructional, transformational, distributed—but no matter what adjective might apply, specific ways in which good leaders achieve the desired impact on student learning have been identified:
- Establishing clear sense of direction—including high expectations and use of data to track progress.
- Developing individual capacity in district personnel through support and professional development.
- Providing instructional guidance.
- Developing and implementing strategic and school improvement plans.
- Making the organization work by addressing all of the conditions that support rather than restrict teaching and learning.

A growing body of evidence indicates that effective schools are most frequently found in school districts that provide strong, system-wide support and guidance. The Council of Great City Schools has identified strategies used in large urban districts that have demonstrated success in raising student performance (Archer, S4):
- Development and implementation of a common curriculum across the district.
- Provision of training in ways to monitor consistent instructional approaches.
- Frequent use of student performance data for instructional and programmatic decision making.

Additional research data indicate the following about the impact of district leadership as well as specific skills that are needed:
- Site-based management has been popular in recent years. Where site-based management has been successful, building leaders have generally had the support and understanding of district administrators.
- While building administrators must be able to develop school improvement plans based on building data and context, district administrators need to be proficient in developing the master plan that encompasses total district needs and is forward-looking (i.e., strategic planning).

A survey commissioned by *Education Week*, with response from more than 800 nationally representative superintendents, identified those practices most commonly used:
- More than 90 percent of superintendents reported that their districts used a common curriculum for all students, that teachers and principals were trained in using performance data, and that instructional walkthroughs were common practice.
- Approximately 80 percent indicated that the same reading and mathematics programs were used district-wide, that the district had a formal training program for teachers new to the district, and that a standard process for writing school improvement plans based on data had been implemented.
- Roughly two-thirds of the districts whose superintendents responded administer their own assessments. While just 60 percent of superintendents reported that instruction is adjusted based on the basis of those local assessments, three-fourths of those leaders felt that the adjustments have had a significant impact on student learning.

Practical implications:
Studies that have focused on the importance of the superintendent's leadership and central office support have found that the central office culture that is most effective is one that is service-oriented rather than regulatory. Specific ways in which central office staff can provide help, in addition to ways already identified in this tip, include the following:
- Establish and follow a specific curriculum review and development cycle.
- Create structures and processes that develop new administrative leadership within the district.

Questions to ask ourselves:
- Have we established within the district common goals that are shared by all stakeholders, including high expectations and opportunities for all students?
- Does our district have common assessments that can be used diagnostically to determine students' status in mastering critical knowledge? If not, what steps can be taken to develop them?
- If assessments are already in place, how are we using the data? What kind of additional staff development is needed to enable teachers to use the data strategically to improve learning for all students?

Resources:
Archer, Jeff. "Theory of Action" and "Guiding Hand." *Education Week* supplement (14 Sept. 2004): S3+.

Leithwood, Kenneth, Karen Louis, Stephen Anderson, and Kyla Wahlstrom. "How Leadership Influences Student Learning." 2004. 15 Mar. 2009 <http://www.wallacefoundation.org/PromoDocs/ReviewofResearchLearningFromLeadership.pdf>.

MacIver, Martha, and Elizabeth Farley-Ripple. *Bringing the District Back In: The Role of the Central Office in Instruction and Achievement*. Alexandria, VA: Educational Research Service, 2008.

RESEARCH TIP #3
Instructional Leadership by Principals

The issue:
What is the influence of educational leadership on children's learning? Researchers have found it to be the second most important school-related factor, with the quality of the teacher in the classroom having the greatest impact on what children learn. With competing demands on their time, building principals need an answer to the question: What does it mean to be an instructional leader?

> The impact of high-quality leadership is usually the greatest in schools with the greatest needs. There are almost no documented cases where schools "in trouble" have made a comeback without the leadership of a strong principal.

The research:
The changing emphasis from building principals as managers to instructional leaders began in the 1980s with the report *A Nation at Risk*. Research on both school and classroom effectiveness identified strong building leadership as a key component to a school's ability to be effective.

The influence that educational leaders have on student learning is indirect. Any leader's impact will depend on the part of the organization to which the leader devotes time and attention. Because teachers are the number-one determiners of student learning, focusing on teachers and classroom instruction gives principals the greatest opportunity to influence student achievement. Focusing on the classroom includes attention to class size, student grouping, instructional practices, and monitoring of student progress.

The phrase "instructional leader" means different things to different people. The most researched educational leadership model is that of Phillip Hallinger, who has identified three critical areas of leadership:
- Establishing the direction in which the school will go—setting a vision, establishing goals and expectations for high performance, and using data to inform decisions.
- Building capacity in people—providing support and training for staff members.
- Developing a climate and culture that promotes rather than restricts the reasons for the school's existence—teaching and learning. No one organizational structure has been found to work better than another; climate and culture are the key ingredients. Leaders who are most successful respond to the context in which they find themselves.

A research summary compiled by Mid-continent Research for Education and Learning included a review of 70 studies aimed at identifying the most critical aspects of a principal's leadership. Components identified were similar to, but not identical with, Hallinger's model and included the following:
- developing school mission and goals that are held by all staff members;
- monitoring effectiveness of programs and practices; and
- involving teachers in making and implementing decisions.

The impact of high-quality leadership is usually the greatest in schools with the greatest needs. There are almost no documented cases where schools "in trouble" have made a comeback without the leadership of a strong principal.

Goldring and associates specifically link research on effective principal leadership to the standards established by the Interstate School Leaders Licensure Consortium (ISLLC). Four of the six ISLLC goals focus on these areas:
- A vision for learning that establishes high expectations that is shared by the school community.
- A culture for learning that is conducive to student achievement as well as professional growth on the part of the faculty; leaders plan, implement, and monitor.
- Support for learning through maintenance of a safe environment and adequate resources.
- Support for learning through involvement of the external community.

The remaining ISLCC goals focus on principal integrity and the policies and regulations within which the principal must operate.

Practical implications:
Analysis by the *Education Week* research department of a recent federal Schools and Staffing Survey provided the following information:
- The vast majority of principals reported they spend time every day on managing security and physical facilities, while just over half indicate they spend time facilitating student learning on a daily basis.
- Fewer than 50 percent of teachers responding to the survey reported that principals talk often with them about instruction.
- While there is no doubt that security is a key issue, principals who are instructional leaders should adjust their schedules so that facilitation of student learning and instructional support of teachers is also a daily feature of their jobs.

Questions to ask ourselves:
- How can I, as a principal, adjust the demands of my schedule to build and support a culture that facilitates student learning?
- How can I, as a principal, build the capacity in staff members that will enable us to work knowledgeably and collaboratively to promote student learning?

Resources:
Archer, Jeff. "Tackling an Impossible Job." *Education Week* supplement (15 Sept. 2004): S3+.

Goldring, Ellen, Andrew C. Porter, Joseph Murphy, Stephen N. Elliott, and Xiu Cravens. "Assessing Learning-Centered Leadership." 2007. 15 Mar. 2009 <http://www.wallacefoundation.org/SiteCollectionDocuments/WF/Knowledge%20Center/Attachments/PDF/Assessing%20Learning-Centered%20Leadership.pdf>.

Hallinger, Phillip. "Research on the Practice of Instructional and Transformational Leadership: Retrospect and Prospect." 2007. 24 July 2008 <http://www.acer.edu.au/documents/RC2007_Hallinger-RetrospectAndProspect.pdf>.

Leithwood, Kenneth, Karen Louis, Stephen Anderson, and Kyla Wahlstrom. "How Leadership Influences Student Learning." 2004. 15 Mar. 2009 <http://www.wallacefoundation.org/PromoDocs/ReviewofResearchLearningFromLeadership.pdf>.

Marzano, Robert, Timothy Waters, and Brian McNulty. *School Leadership that Works: From Research to Results*. Arlington, VA: Association for Supervision and Curriculum Development, 2005.

RESEARCH TIP #4
Teachers as Leaders

The issue:
The previous research tip as well as Tip #7 address the increasing demands on principals, while the number of hours available to meet these demands remains unchanged. Both tips ask principals to consider how they might increase capacity among staff members and use that expertise to lighten the load in leading educational efforts within a building. Author Charlotte Danielson holds that "teacher leadership is an idea whose time has come." What does literature tell us about the impact and utilization of teacher leadership?

> Many teacher leaders are individuals who hold no official leadership role but who influence decision making and are looked to by colleagues for advice and counsel.

The research:
Studies on the impact of teacher leadership on student achievement are limited and provide conflicting results.
- Qualitative studies suggest that teachers as leaders have a positive influence on students' academic achievement, but only a few quantitative studies have been conducted that address this question. Those studies have found no correlation between teacher leadership and student achievement.
- A state-wide study of schools in Kentucky that were being successful in closing the achievement gap identified common practices in those schools. One of those practices was the presence of teacher leadership, which was encouraged and expected—specifically in the areas of school-wide improvement and student achievement.
- Teacher leadership can be both formal and informal.
- Many teacher leaders are individuals who hold no official leadership role but who influence decision making and are looked to by colleagues for advice and counsel.
- Formal leadership can occur in multiple ways, including but not limited to the following: department chair or grade-level team leader, vertical team leader, instructional coach, mentor, professional development presenter, and school improvement team leader or participant.

Reasons why teachers are becoming leaders include the following:
- Increased emphasis on accountability has led principals to depend more and more on the expertise of classroom teachers in raising student achievement.
- Teacher leaders welcome the opportunity for more interaction and less isolation.
- Teacher leaders can take on different responsibilities and expand their sphere of influence.

Results from a 2003 survey of teachers recognized as accomplished teachers (Presidential Math and Science Awardees, Teachers of the Year, National Board-Certified Teachers) provide insight into how these recognized teachers perceive themselves as leaders:
- Almost all of these teachers considered themselves as leaders and believed that their colleagues viewed them in that light as well.
- The teachers reported that their leadership was manifested in a variety of ways: professional development, curriculum development, mentoring, and leading departments or grade-level teams.

These same teachers indicated areas in which they felt personal needs:
- Recognized teachers are being asked to assume roles for which they have not been prepared; working with adults requires a different skill set than working with students.
- The teachers would like new leadership roles, including recruitment of new teachers and input on educational policies and decisions, with appropriate training for the demands of those roles.

Practical implications:
Obstacles for being a teacher leader, as described by teachers who have assumed the role, include the following:
- A school structure that did not change to maximize the potential of teachers as leaders.
- A lack of precise definitions of what a teacher leader's role should be.
- Resistance from some teachers for support and/or coaching from a colleague who has assumed the role of teacher leader.

The position taken by a principal regarding teacher leaders in his or her building is critical. The principal can define the roles for designated leaders in specific situations and can work toward developing a culture in which the expertise of teacher leaders is appreciated and accepted.

Questions to ask ourselves:
- Do I, as an individual, accept leadership roles that use my personal strengths and expertise? Do I respect and accept the assistance provided by my colleagues who are teacher leaders?
- How can we, as a building staff, strengthen and utilize the leadership capacity of all our staff members?
- Do I, as the principal in my building, depend on the professionals on my staff to lead in a variety of ways? Do I give them the support necessary to assume those leadership roles, including the appropriate professional development?

Resources:
Danielson, Charlotte. "Strengthening the School's Backbone." *Journal for Staff Development* (Spring 2005): 34-37.

Dozier, Terry. "Turning Good Teachers into Great Leaders." *Educational Leadership* (Sept. 2007): 14-19.

Gabriel, John. *How to Thrive as a Teacher Leader*. Arlington, VA: Association for Supervision and Curriculum Development, 2005.

Johnson, Susan, and Morgaen Donaldson. "Overcoming the Obstacles to Leadership." *Educational Leadership* (Sept. 2007): 8-13.

Laine, Jaynae, and Debbie Hickst. "Common Threads Found among Schools Closing Achievement Gaps." 2008. 15 Mar. 2009 <http://www.kltprc.net/foresight/Chpt_97.htm>.

Wynne, Joan. "Teachers as Leaders in Education Reform." Undated. 25 June 2008 <http://www.ericdigests.org/2002-4/teachers.html>.

RESEARCH TIP #5
Effective Staff Meetings

The issue:
The beginning of a new school year is an ideal time to consider the design of faculty meetings. Staff developer Joan Richardson writes, "Almost any teacher or principal would agree that faculty meetings are one of the most dreaded and ineffective parts of the work week." While empirical data about good and bad meetings are scarce, there is an abundance of qualitative data. This research tip will focus on effective meetings in general, while the following tip will address staff development norms and protocols that can enhance faculty meetings.

> A key to productive staff meetings is a supportive culture that is school-wide, so staff members are comfortable raising issues and voicing opinions during faculty meetings.

The research:
Common complaints about faculty meetings include the following:
- information could have been shared some other way;
- timing was bad (before school, after school, teachers tired, coaches absent); and
- issues are addressed in a context (committee of whole) that has the least chance of solving a problem.

Education World provides a lengthy list of tips about "Great Meetings." Some of the ideas from that list include the following:
- Determine whether or not a meeting is really necessary. Is interaction necessary? Call a meeting. Is information to be shared? Write a bulletin or memo.
- Plan for a strong opening and a strong closing, with both emphasizing the purpose of the meeting and the associated tasks. The opening includes an agenda for the meeting, while the closing ends the meeting with decisions made and tasks and responsibilities assigned as need be.
- Stay on task. Have a "parking lot" to record ideas that are important but off-topic from the agenda.

Best practices for leading effective meetings in any venue have been identified:
- start and end on time;
- have a clearly defined purpose for the meeting;
- develop an agenda that leads to action;
- designate specific time limits for agenda items;
- agree on norms or protocols for meeting behavior;
- delineate responsibilities for key roles, such as recorder and timekeeper;
- use a flipchart or projector to create a visual record during the meeting; and
- establish a process for evaluating meetings.

Practical implications:
While best practices have been identified, so have common problems with possible solutions.

Problem	Possible Solution
Meetings don't end on time.	Start on time; plan timing of agenda items in advance; have a timekeeper.
The group can't make a decision.	Create expectation for actions with the agenda; prioritize possible actions; look for data that support specific action.
Some folks dominate, while others are silent.	Structure the conversation with specific questions to consider; break a large group into smaller groups where quiet folks are more apt to speak.
Decisions are often revisited during the meeting.	Keep records of past decisions as well as displaying visual record of current meeting; involve all members in discussion.
Minor issues take too much time, reducing time available for major ones.	Break larger issues into manageable parts; allow time in meeting plan for significant issues while limiting time for minor ones.
Follow-through after meetings is lacking.	End meetings with a written action plan; leader checks on progress between meetings.

- A key to productive staff meetings is a supportive culture that is school-wide, so staff members are comfortable raising issues and voicing opinions during faculty meetings.
- The building principal, especially one new to a building or one who is seeking to initiate change, is a key player in fostering the development of such a culture.

Questions to ask ourselves:
- How can we best share routine information without detracting from valuable meeting time?
- What are the most important things we wish to focus on in this year's faculty meetings?
- What specific steps can we take to help ensure follow-through between meetings?
- Am I personally a dominator or a silent participant? How can I improve my own participation?

Resources:
Bassett, Patrick. "Faculty Meeting Blues." 1996. 22 Apr. 2008 <http://www.isacs.org/resources/monographs/library.asp?id=241&category=11&action=show>.

Delisio, Ellen. "Organizing Staff Meetings Even *You* Want to Attend." 2008. 22 Apr. 2008 <http://www.education-world.com/a_admin/admin/admin518.shtml>.

Education World. "Great Meetings." Undated. 22 Apr. 2008 <http://www.education-world.com/a_admin/archives/greatmeetings.shtml>.

Richardson, Joan. "Harness the Potential of Staff Meetings." Oct. 1999. 15 Mar. 2009 <http://www.nsdc.org/news/tools/tools10-99rich.cfm>.

RESEARCH TIP #6
Staff Meetings as Professional Development

The issue:
The previous research tip talked in broad terms about effective meeting management. This tip addresses faculty meetings focused on staff development, including norms and protocols for such meetings. The emphasis is on collaborative faculty meetings during which staff members look at student work or engage in book studies.

> Book studies can help faculties make decisions about where to focus their time and energy in a way that will benefit the students in their respective buildings.

The research:
Norms and protocols are two words found frequently in literature about collaborative faculty work. The difference between the two terms is one of nuances:
- Norms tend to be more general and address behaviors between and among participants regardless of the content of the meeting. Norms focus on mutual respect and interaction and are created to fit the needs and concerns of the faculty involved.
- A protocol is more specific and provides a structure, including both processes and time allotted to specific processes, that creates a safe environment for discussion. Some of the most widely used protocols relate to Looking at Student Work (LASW).

LASW is an effective staff development strategy that provides multiple benefits:
- It helps teachers analyze the quality of the assignments they are giving to students, both in alignment with grade-level curriculum and the rigor of the assignment.
- It provides teachers with additional information for helping individual students improve.
- It improves the effectiveness of classroom instruction.

Data from large-scale analyses of student work provide the following information:
- DataWorks, in a study of more than 30,000 student assignments, found that the alignment between assigned student work and California's English/Language Arts academic standards was 100 percent at kindergarten but decreased each year to less than 30 percent at the junior-senior level.
- A review of 1,400 work samples from Chicago Public School students revealed that 70 percent of those samples presented either no challenge or minimal challenge. However, when students were presented with a greater challenge, the quality of their work was much higher.
- The data from analysis, with action based on those data, can make a difference. Trend data from individual schools in which faculty members analyzed the relationship between teacher assignments and grade-level standards showed a dramatic increase in the percentage of grade-level assignments from one year to the next as well as improvement on high-stakes external assessments.

Principals and teachers have found book studies to be an additional way to spend meeting time in a way that builds their professional knowledge and increases their repertoire of skills.
- Book studies can shape direction for change in a nonthreatening manner.

- Book studies can help faculties make decisions about where to focus their time and energy in a way that will benefit the students in their respective buildings.
- Book studies have been found to make a difference in student performance in typically low-performing urban elementary schools.
- Identification of books for study can begin with teachers or principals. Best results occur when a book chosen supports the needs or school improvement goals of the school in which teachers are working.
- Some schools and districts have made book study a required part of their professional development efforts, while others have made book study a strictly voluntary affair.

Practical implications:

Practitioners who have chosen to restructure faculty meetings and use those meetings as a part of the overall staff development plan within their respective buildings have found that focus is important to teachers. Teachers prefer to spend extended time with a particular topic or routine, rather than responding to a shotgun approach that changes with each meeting.

Looking at Student Work and book studies both require collaboration to be successful. The approach for collaboration at any given school will vary according to the staff's degree of readiness. Staff developers suggest the following differentiated approaches:
- Little collaboration in place: Begin with nonthreatening activities such as sharing of ideas and materials.
- Moderate collaboration: Invite teachers to submit (anonymously) a problem that can be discussed in a faculty meeting. A teacher whose problem is discussed can leave a meeting with multiple ideas of how to address the issues.
- Strong collaboration: Introduce faculty members to the concept of analyzing assignments—both the tasks given to students and the quality of responses that students bring to those tasks.

Questions to ask ourselves:
- What is our degree of readiness, as a school faculty, for collaborative activities?
- What kind of help do we need to begin the process of Looking at Student Work?
- How can we identify and select books for book study that will be most relevant to us and the students we teach?

Resources:

The Education Trust. "Effects of Student Achievement by Teachers in SIP Teams." 2007. 30 July 2008 <http://www2.edtrust.org/EdTrust/SIP+Professional+Development/ Standards+in+practice+2.htm>.

Dunne, Diane. "Teachers Learn from Looking Together at Student Work." 2000. 30 July 2008 <http://www.education-world.com/a_curr/curr246.html>.

Hollingsworth, John. Data Works Professional Development Conference for Principals. Los Angeles Unified School District, Sept. 2002.

Keller, Bess. "'Book Study' Helps Teachers Hone Skills." *Education Week* (21 May 2008): 1+.

Looking at Student Work. "Protocols." Undated. 30 July 2008 <http://www.lasw.org/protocols.html>.

Richardson, Joan. "Harness the Potential of Staff Meetings." 15 Mar. 2009 <http://www.nsdc.org/ news/tools/tools10-99rich.cfm>.

RESEARCH TIP #7
Time Management Tips for Principals

The issue:
Long days are a fact of life for school principals. A decade-long survey by the National Association of Elementary School Principals, completed in 1998, found that the average elementary principal spent 58 hours a week at work or on work-related tasks. A more recent study completed by McPeake in 2006 found that time dedicated to the job by principals at all levels (elementary through high school) has risen from 49 hours in the 1960s to 61 hours in the current decade. Clearly, managing time is an important skill for administrators. What does research tell us about factors influencing time management, and what are some of the tricks-of-the-trade that work?

> Presence in the classroom, in the hallways, and at student activities often alerts administrators to developing problems in time to keep small issues from escalating into big ones. Administrative presence in a variety of venues also provides the opportunity for communication with students, staff, and parents.

The research:
A 1990 study by Furman found very different perspectives between school principals and district superintendents on how principals should spend their time. Principals listed activities by actual time expenditure from the most time-consuming to the least time-consuming, while superintendents listed activities by how they believed principals should be spending their time.

Priority	Principals (actual time spent)	Superintendents (expectations of principals)
1	Paperwork	Instructional supervision
2	Meetings	Curriculum activities
3	Disciplinary issues	Conferences with teachers and staff
4	Cafeteria duty	Meetings
5	Parental issues (including conferences)	Parental issues (including conferences)
6	Conferences with teachers and staff	Disciplinary issues
7	Curriculum activities	Paperwork
8	Instructional supervision	Cafeteria duty

Because these data are almost two decades old, practicing administrators may feel they do not represent today's educational scenarios. Data collected by Downey present a different approach in that the data reflect where (by location) principals themselves say they spend their time. Data collected from 13 different studies revealed the following:
- 40-80 percent of principals' time is spent in the office or office area
- 23-40 percent of the time is spent in hallways and playground
- 11 percent is spent off campus
- 2.5-10 percent is spent in classrooms

Practical implications:
If principals are to be instructional leaders, somewhere time must be found to supervise curriculum and instruction. Tried-and-true strategies for managing time come from both the business world and practicing administrators who have successfully implemented certain practices.
- Set priorities. These are not the same for everyone. Some principals list curriculum and instruction as their number one priority, while others list student safety. Those issues that are most important and that should require the most time devoted to them should be at the top of any principal's priority list.
- Plan. The importance of planning can be found on the "to do" list of almost any time management expert. According to one author, "One minute of planning can save 20 minutes of doing" (Hopkins, p. 6).
- Develop a running "to do" list. Such a list should reflect individual priorities and be evidence of that individual's planning. It also provides terrific reinforcement as tasks are checked off when completed.
- Delegate. One person cannot do it all. Trust individuals—secretaries, teachers, other administrators—to do their jobs. In addition, a leadership team can provide input in a variety of ways and members of the team will often volunteer to take on the responsibility for seeing a task through to the finish.
- Learn to say "No." Some tasks do not need to be delegated; they simply need to be refused initially. A good question to ask one's self when considering whether or not to accept a new responsibility: "Will this make a difference for my staff or my students?"
- Be visible. Presence in the classroom, in the hallways, and at student activities often alerts administrators to developing problems in time to keep small issues from escalating into big ones. Administrative presence in a variety of venues also provides the opportunity for communication with students, staff, and parents.

Questions to ask myself:
- Have I established my personal goals so that I can prioritize my time to reflect those goals?
- Do I know how I spend my day? How can I collect that data so I might use my time more effectively?
- Do I effectively use the individuals with whom I work on a regular basis to lighten my load as well as make the school run more smoothly and efficiently?

Resources:
Downey, Carolyn. *Participant's Manual. Conducting Walkthroughs to Maximize Student Achievement: Cutting Edge Practice Series.* Johnson, IA: Curriculum Management Services, Inc., 2001.

Furman, Robert, and Richard Zibrida. "The Hurried Principal." 1990. 02 June 2008 <http://eric.ed.gov/ERICDocs/data/ericdocs2sql/content_storage_01/0000019b/80/13/45/7e.pdf>.

Hopkins, Gary. "Principals Offer Practical, Timely 'Time Management' Tips." Jan. 2006. 02 June 2008 <http://www.educationworld.com/a_admin/admin/admin436_a.shtml>.

Magnuson, Peter. "Finding Time." *Communicator* (Mar. 2003): 1+. 15 Mar. 2009 <http://www.aypsupport.org/DetroitFallInstitute_files/FindingTime.pdf>.

McPeake, Jacqueline. "The Principalship: A Study of the Principal's Time on Task from 1960 to the Twenty-First Century." 2006. 02 June 2008 <http://www.marshall.edu/etd/doctors/mcpeake-jaqueline-2007-phd.pdf>.

Section II: Meeting the Needs of All Children

RESEARCH TIP #8
Differentiation

The issue:
Differentiated instruction is a mixture of theories and practices for teaching that are based on the belief that instructional strategies should reflect the individual and diverse needs of students in a given classroom. Use of differentiated instruction has become an expectation in classrooms across the country. Rather than "teaching to the middle," teachers are expected to find activities and assessments that match student interests and abilities. At the same time, teachers are expected to hold all students accountable for the content they are expected to master for high-stakes assessments. All of this is a daunting task. What does research tell us about the effects of differentiation, and what does differentiated instruction look like?

> Differentiated instruction is student-centered. It builds student understanding on previous learning and a realization that not all students possess the same backgrounds and abilities.

The research:
Empirical data on the effects of differentiated instruction per se are lacking. Research data that are available support some of the underlying premises of differentiation:
- Differentiation is intended to engage each student at an appropriate level for his or her learning. Academic learning time has been defined as that subset of time-on-task when each student is experiencing success at a task at the appropriate level of difficulty (Nichols, p. 6). Academic learning time has been found to be more beneficial for student learning than simply time-on-task.
- Differentiation aims to provide learning experiences at which all students can be reasonably successful. In classrooms studied where students performed at about 80 percent accuracy, students learned more and felt better about themselves.
- Grouping can be a component of differentiation, though it need not be part of every differentiated activity. Grouping students for instruction has been supported by research data as an effective practice.

Qualitative findings presented in studies of classrooms where differentiated instruction is occurring include the following:
- Differentiated instruction provides multiple approaches to content, process, product, and assessment and provides a blend of whole-class, group, and individual instruction.
- Teachers in differentiated classrooms begin with a clear and solid sense of what constitutes appropriate curriculum and engaging instruction.
- Differentiated instruction is proactive with teachers planning a variety of ways to involve students and allow them to express their learning.
- Differentiated classrooms provide a focus on how individual students learn and how they demonstrate what they have learned.
- Differentiated instruction is student-centered. It builds student understanding on previous learning and a realization that not all students possess the same backgrounds and abilities.
- Teachers in differentiated classrooms give their students as much responsibility for their learning as possible and engage their students in talking about classroom procedures and group processes.

- Differentiated classrooms provide students with options in addressing project assignments. These assignments should ensure that students rethink ideas and information previously studied.
- Teachers using differentiated instruction provide several options, but they do not develop a separate lesson plan for every student.
- Teachers who differentiate their instruction provide challenges at an appropriate level so that all students have the opportunity to master expected curricular objectives; teachers do not "water down" the curriculum.
- Beginning teachers may need time to learn the basic fundamentals of teaching and classroom management before they are ready to address differentiation in their classrooms.

Practical implications:
- Offer students a variety of options for the creation of a final product. Base options on the students' interests so they can link what they have learned with something that matters to them individually.
- Use time flexibly; incorporate a range of instructional strategies to ensure that the learning and learning environment are shaped to the learners.
- Provide lessons for all students that emphasize critical thinking and engagement with learning.
- Design new learning based on an assessment of prior student knowledge, not on the assumption that students already possess content knowledge.
- Match homework to the students with a goal of ensuring that practice is meaningful for all.
- In lieu of whole group instruction, use a series of direct instruction sessions that includes practice and application groups.

Questions to ask ourselves:
- Is there a staff development plan in place to support teachers as they work with differentiated instructional techniques?
- Is there a parent communication plan to prepare parents and students for instruction in a differentiated classroom?
- Is there an assessment plan in place that includes a variety of assessment options to evaluate student assignments and products?

Resources:
Glencoe. "Differentiating Instruction: Meeting Students Where They Are." Undated. 24 Mar. 2008 <http://www.glencoe.com/sec/teachingtoday/subject/di_meeting.phtml>.

Gould, Holly. "Can Novice Teachers Differentiate Instruction? Yes, They CAN!" 2004. 24 Mar. 2008 <http://newhorizons.org/strategies/differentiated/gould.htm>.

Hall, Tracey. "Differentiated Instruction." Undated. 24 Mar. 2008 <http://www.cast.org/publications/ncac/ncac_diffinstructudl.html>.

Nichols, Beverly. *Improving Student Achievement: 50 Research-Based Strategies.* Columbus, OH: Linworth Publishing, Inc., 2008.

Tomlinson, Carol Ann. *The Differentiated Classroom: Responding to the Needs of All Learners.* Alexandria, VA: Association for Supervision and Curriculum Development, 1999.

RESEARCH TIP #9
Autism

The issue:
Autism is more prevalent among children than disorders that are better known, such as diabetes or Down syndrome. Recent studies indicate that three out of every 1,000 children between the ages of three and 10 may suffer from autism. More than half of these children are not diagnosed before entering kindergarten. Current estimates indicate that nearly four million children will be diagnosed with autism within the next 10 years. What are the implications for educators as they seek to meet the needs of autistic students?

> Individuals with autism are not retarded or incapable of learning; however, some students may have difficulty expressing what they know.

The research:
Autism affects boys more than girls by a ratio of four to one. All children with autism spectrum disorders, regardless of gender, have deficiencies in three areas: social interactions; communication, both verbal and nonverbal; and repetitive behaviors. These symptoms, which may run from mild to severe, exhibit themselves differently in individual children. Specific behaviors related to each of these areas include the following.

Social interactions:
- Children may resist attention and physical contact.
- Autistic children have difficulty interpreting the feelings of others, including cues such as smiles or frowns. As a result, they are often unable to understand actions of others.
- They frequently avoid eye contact, but it is a misconception to believe they cannot make eye contact.
- Some autistic individuals have trouble controlling emotions; this difficulty may result in outbursts or disruptive behavior.

Communication:
- Speech development may be delayed. In extreme cases, individuals suffering from autism remain mute for their entire lives.
- Words and language are often used differently. Words may not be combined into meaningful sentences, or the same words may be used over and over. Children with large vocabularies may not be able to sustain meaningful conversation.
- Nonverbal communication, such as gestures and facial expressions, may not match what children are saying.

Repetitive behavior:
- Even though children with autism may appear physically normal, they may exhibit repetitive motions such as flapping their arms, or they may freeze in place.
- Repetition may be exhibited through intense preoccupation with a single object or topic.

Certain myths about autism need to be refuted in order to meet the needs of autistic children in our schools:
- Autistic children are not necessarily savants or geniuses. In some instances they may

demonstrate unusual capabilities in a given area, but this is not a given condition of autism.
- On the other hand, individuals with autism are not retarded or incapable of learning; however, some students may have difficulty expressing what they know.
- Autistic students are not antisocial, but they may need assistance in learning how to communicate for social interaction. They have emotional bonds with family members, teachers, and friends but may have difficulty expressing their feelings.

Practical implications:
What does research tell us about meeting the needs of autistic children?
- Children suffering from autism spectrum disorders need consistency. Changes in routine can be confusing and disturbing.
- Television and videos, used appropriately, can be excellent tools in teaching skills and emotional responses. Using videos allows the repetition that meets the needs of many children.
- Teachers who have autistic children in their classrooms as part of a least restrictive environment need specific training in meeting the needs of autistic children.
- Classroom accommodations that support the learning needs of autistic children are similar in many ways to the accommodations for children with other needs: limiting the size of a task or breaking a larger task into smaller pieces; adjusting the time allowed for learning or for completing a task; and providing additional support through teaching assistants, peer tutors, or learning buddies.
- The placement of an autistic child's desk or seat in the classroom is important. Noises coming from other children located behind an autistic child can interfere with attention or concentration.

Teachers who have worked with autistic children recommend meeting with parents before the school year begins to gain more knowledge about the individual child. In addition, having the child visit the classroom several times before the school year starts helps in establishing familiarity and routine.

Questions to ask ourselves:
- Have we as a faculty had training in recognizing the symptoms of autism? Are we aware of the various forms of treatment and the pros and cons of each?
- Have our classroom teachers as well as teachers in the library, the gym, and other special areas received staff development in meeting the needs of the specific children whom they teach each day?

Resources:
Autism Research Institute. "Developing Academic Accommodations Promoting Successful Inclusion." 2007. 18 Aug. 2008 <http://www.autism.com/individuals/9domains.htm>.
Franklin, John. "Achieving with Autism." *Education Update*. Association for Supervision and Curriculum Development (July 2007): 1+.
National Institute of Mental Health. *Autism Spectrum Disorders (Pervasive Developmental Disorders)*. 2007. 18 Aug. 2008 <http://www.nimh.nih.gov/health/publications/autism/nimhautismspectrum.pdf>.
Rudy, Lisa Jo. *Your Guide to Autism*. 2007. 17 Nov. 2007 <http://autism.about.com>.

RESEARCH TIP #10
Dyslexia

The issue:
The International Dyslexia Association formally defines dyslexia as "a neurologically-based disorder, often familial, which interferes with the acquisition and processing of language." A more simple definition from Bright Solutions states that "Dyslexia is an inherited condition that makes it extremely difficult to read, write, and spell in your native language—despite at least average intelligence." What is the extent of dyslexia, and what should principals and classroom teachers know about the disorder?

> Over 180 research studies to date have proven that phonics is the BEST WAY to teach reading to all students. They also have shown that phonics is the ONLY WAY to teach reading to students with dyslexia and other learning disabilities.

The research:
Individuals and organizations who study dyslexia cite different figures regarding the extent of dyslexia:
- The Child Development Institute estimates that 3-6 percent of the population is affected by true dyslexia. Many children who have learning disabilities are not dyslexic.
- The International Dyslexia Association estimates that 15-20 percent of the population as a whole has some symptoms of dyslexia. Not all of these individuals would qualify for special education services during their school days, but all would benefit from explicit instruction and appropriate interventions in learning language skills.

While there may be disagreement on the extent of the problem, there is considerable agreement about symptoms and ways to address the condition once it is diagnosed:
- Dyslexia is an inherited, neurological condition. It is a lifelong condition, but many dyslexics learn to read and write well.
- The brain's right hemisphere is larger in dyslexics; as a result, individuals with dyslexia often demonstrate particular skills in areas controlled by the right side of the brain, such as artistic, athletic, and mechanical skills.
- Dyslexia can affect different functions:
  > Visual dyslexia manifests itself in the reversal of numbers and letters and the inability to write numbers and letters in the correct sequence.
  > Auditory dyslexia results in difficulty in hearing the sounds of letters or groups of letters; in auditory reception the sounds may be jumbled or heard incorrectly.
  > Dysgraphia may apply to a child who has ongoing difficulty holding and controlling a pencil in order to make correct markings on paper.
- While problems with dyslexia may be most pronounced in reading, individuals with dyslexia also may have problems with spelling and writing.
- Researchers at the National Health Institute have identified phonemic awareness as the most important factor that determines whether or not a student can read normally or be classified as a disabled reader.
- The Child Development Institute has built on this finding with the following strong statement: "Over 180 research studies to date have proven that phonics is the BEST WAY to teach reading to all students. They also have shown that phonics is the ONLY

WAY to teach reading to students with dyslexia and other learning disabilities" (Child Development Institute, p. 2.).
- Most people with dyslexia have problems with phonemic awareness, i.e. identifying the separate speech sounds within a word or identifying how letters represent these sounds.
- Phonemic awareness must be explicitly taught before phonics instruction will make sense to a child.
- The Response to Intervention (RTI) process may serve as a tool for early identification of children with dyslexia. (See Tip #13.)
- Students with dyslexia may have emotional problems resulting from frustration; as a result, they may need counseling to help them cope.

Practical implications:
- There is no immediate or easy solution for dyslexia. It can take from one to three years to get a child up to grade level in reading and spelling, depending upon severity and type of interventions.
- Dyslexic children need explicit instruction in phonemic awareness, how to break a word or syllable into individual sounds, and how to take individual sounds and blend them into a word. Once sounds can be differentiated, children need to know which letters correspond to specific sounds.
- Individuals with dyslexia need to be taught with explicit, systematic methods that use multiple senses at the same time or in close proximity. A child might see a letter, hear its name and sound, and write the letter in the air—all at the same time.
- Dyslexic children need specific instruction, one rule at a time, with frequent and intense practice in order to master the rule.
- Dyslexic children need to have rules and processes already learned reviewed regularly and integrated into current lessons. This is important for all children, but essential for ones who are dyslexic.

Questions to ask ourselves:
- What processes do we have in place, such as RTI, to identify children with dyslexia at an early age and grade?
- Do we have an appropriate program in place to teach phonemic awareness first, and then phonics?
- What kind of additional support systems do we have in place to meet the needs of dyslexic children as well as other children with reading difficulties?

Resources:
Bright Solutions for Dyslexia, LLC. "Teaching Methods That Work." 1998. 23 Aug. 2008 <http://www.dys-add.com/teach.html>.
Bright Solutions for Dyslexia, LLC. "What Is Dyslexia?" 1998. 23 Aug. 2008 <http://www.dys-add.com/define.html>.
Child Development Institute. "About Dyslexia & Reading Problems." Undated. 23 Aug. 2008 <http://www.childdevelopmentinfo.com/learning/dyslexia.shtml>.
International Dyslexia Association. "Dyslexia Basics." 2008. 23 Aug. 2008 <http://www.interdys.org/ewebeditpro5/upload/Basics_Fact_Sheet_5-08-08.pdf>.
MedicineNet, Inc. "Dyslexia." 2002. 23 Aug. 2008 <http://www.medicinenet.com/dyslexia/article.htm>.

RESEARCH TIP #11
ADD-ADHD

The issue:
Many children with Attention Deficit Disorder (ADD) or Attention Deficit/Hyperactivity Disorder (ADHD) are not identified until they enter school. At that point a child's impulsivity, lack of attention, and hyperactivity become apparent as they interfere with learning. What should teachers look for in identifying these disorders? Once ADD or ADHD is diagnosed, how can school personnel be most effective in helping students deal with the challenges of the disorders?

> About 60 percent of children who are diagnosed have the condition as adults. Adults who have been successful in managing ADD or ADHD say the most important factor in their success was that someone believed in them.

The research:
Three to seven percent of school-age children suffer from ADD/ADHD. These children generally exhibit symptoms in preschool or early elementary school, and symptoms may continue throughout life. Boys are three times more likely than girls to be diagnosed. The American Psychological Association has certain criteria for diagnosing a child with ADD/ADHD:
- Inattention: frequently fails to finish something started, is easily distracted, has difficulty concentrating on schoolwork or sticking to a play activity.
- Impulsiveness: has difficulty waiting turn in games, calls out in class, acts without thinking, changes frequently from one activity to another, has difficulty organizing.
- Hyperactivity: has difficulty staying seated, fidgets while seated, runs around or climbs on things excessively.

Usually these symptoms are manifest before the age of seven but should be observed for a period of at least six months before a diagnosis of ADD.

According to the Chesapeake Institute, schools that are successful in meeting the needs of ADD/ADHD children recognize that "students with ADD are not problem children, but rather children with a problem." Services provided by these schools may include the following:
- Staff members recognize that children with ADD/ADHD are not a homogeneous group and work to provide services that reflect the individual needs of each child.
- The teaching of social skills to ADD/ADHD students helps in reducing the rejection of ADD/ADHD students by their non-ADD peers.
- School personnel work together with parents to establish consistent or complementary processes and routines for home and school.

Practical implications:
Teacher activities and strategies for meeting the academic needs of children diagnosed with ADD or ADHD include, but are not limited to, the following:
- Design academic tasks so they are clear and manageable. This may include breaking an assignment down into smaller parts that fit a student's attention span.
- Place an ADD student's desk near the teacher's desk or in the front row to help focus attention. (This placement is the opposite of that recommended for a student with autism.)
- Have the student put away any unnecessary or distracting materials when working on a particular task.

- Give ADD students advance warning when a transition in activities is eminent. Provide clear and consistent directions for transition times.
- Use the child's name before addressing a question to an ADD child. This allows the child to focus his or her attention on the question.
- Plan activities with variety, such as hands-on activities with manipulatives, activities that require more physical activity, or a change in stimuli such as colored paper.
- Multistep directions are difficult for ADD/ADHD students to follow. Break directions into parts that are brief and specific, with visual prompts as well as oral ones.
- Academic instruction is most effective in the morning, because on-task behavior of ADHD students deteriorates during the day. Elementary teachers can plan schedules so that more demanding tasks occur in the morning. At the secondary level, counselors can plan a student's schedule so classes with more rigorous demands occur earlier in the day.
- ADD/ADHD students benefit from specific instruction in note taking. Partial outlines that require students to complete the outlines while listening or reading can be helpful.

Successful strategies for managing classroom behavior include the following:
- Establish specific rules (few in number) with immediate consequences when the rules are broken. Communicate expectations and rules clearly and explicitly.
- Implement a behavior management system in which rewards are given for good behavior.
- Work on a few behaviors at a time rather than trying to manage a wide spectrum of behavioral issues.
- Interventions should target specific behaviors. When an inappropriate behavior is identified, an appropriate alternative should be chosen to replace that problem behavior.

About 60 percent of children who are diagnosed have the condition as adults. Adults who have been successful in managing ADD or ADHD say the most important factor in their success was that someone believed in them.

Questions to ask ourselves:
- Do we, as a school faculty, have a school-wide plan for meeting the needs of all students diagnosed with ADD or ADHD? Does this plan enable classroom teachers to meet individual needs as well?
- What kind of staff development do we need to effectively meet the needs of individual children diagnosed with ADD/ADHD?
- Do I, as a classroom teacher, demonstrate to my ADD/ADHD students that I believe in them and their ability to succeed?

Resources:
Brock, Stephen. "Special Needs: Helping the Student with ADHD in the Classroom." 2002. 21 Aug. 2008 <http://www.nasponline.org/resources/handouts/special%20needs%20template.pdf>.
Chesapeake Institute. "Attention Deficit Disorder: What Teachers Should Know." Undated. 21 Aug. 2008 <http://user.cybrzn.com/kenyonck/add/doe_tch.htm>.
DuPaul, George, and George White. "An ADHD Primer." *Principal Leadership Magazine* (Oct. 2004): 1+. 21 Aug. 2008 <http://www.nasponline.org/resources/principals/nassp_adhd.aspx>.
Scott, Mary. "Attention Deficit Disorder (ADD). Digest #445." 1987. 21 Aug. 2008 <http://www.ericdigests.org/pre-927/add.htm>.

RESEARCH TIP #12
Success with Hispanic Students

The issue:
There are an estimated five million English language learners (ELLs) in the nation, based on data reported by state departments of education. Hispanic students comprise almost 75 percent of this student group. The achievement gap between Hispanic students and non-Hispanic white students is well documented. In addition, the dropout rate for Hispanic students is 2.5 times greater than the rate for all students. Some schools, however, are demonstrating unexpected success in raising the achievement level of Hispanic students. Furthermore, research has identified specific strategies that work well with all ELL students, including Hispanics. What are the characteristics of these successful schools? What strategies are helpful?

> What was consistent was the fact that schools selected a program based on students' needs, trained teachers in implementation of the program, then stuck with it rather than changing programs over time.

The research:
The Morrison Institute for Public Policy at Arizona State University adapted the methodology used by Jim Collins in *Good to Great: Why Some Companies Make the Leap ... and Others Don't* in a study of Arizona schools serving large numbers of poor and Hispanic children. Twelve elementary and middle schools were identified in which the children were "beating the odds." These schools were schools in which students performed better than expected over time, often scoring above state averages, or schools that made steady improvements over the time frame for which data was available. After identifying the schools, researchers looked for those characteristics that were present in the successful schools but missing in the comparison schools with similar demographics. Six characteristics were identified. Some of these characteristics are similar to ones found in effective schools research; others are more specific to this set of schools.

- Personnel focused on the performance of each classroom and every student in that classroom. All staff members at these schools assumed responsibility for individual student achievement.
- A variety of data was reviewed on an ongoing basis, rather than depending on data from once-a-year high stakes assessments. Teachers and principals used regular assessments to measure performance and identify problems; they then took steps to address the problem areas.
- Strong principals worked with teachers, both as leaders and side-by-side with the teachers to bring about improvement. Principals held high expectations for students in their schools and did not make excuses based on demographics.
- Staff members accepted responsibility for school improvement and collaborated with one another in identifying problems, then implementing solutions.
- Programs used by the successful schools were varied; no one program was identified as a silver bullet. What was consistent was the fact that schools selected a program based on students' needs, trained teachers in implementation of the program, then stuck with it rather than changing programs over time.
- The successful schools knew how to differentiate. Teachers planned instruction and interventions based on specific needs of students—both as a group and as individuals.

Additional findings from the study included the following:
- There was little turnover in building leadership at the successful schools. Principal changes at comparison schools were much more frequent. There was little difference, however, in teacher turnover at the successful schools and the comparison schools.
- The degree of parental involvement was not an issue; parental involvement was very similar at both successful and comparison schools.
- There were no differences between the two sets of schools—successful vs. comparison—in areas which are often the culprits for lack of success. The factors that were similar across schools included class size, money, teacher qualifications, and length of the school day and year.

Practical implications:

Research results are mixed when bilingual instruction is compared with English-only immersion. Good practices are less controversial and apply to Hispanic students as well as other ELL students. A partial list of these strategies includes the following:
- Have high expectations and communicate those expectations. At the same time, provide support in a variety of ways.
- Don't talk down to students. Speak slowly, but don't oversimplify. Don't confuse talking loudly with explaining clearly.
- Be well informed about students and their backgrounds, their interests, and their skills. Use this knowledge to connect current instruction with prior knowledge or student culture. (See Tip #46.)
- Encourage reading on a regular basis. This builds vocabulary and background knowledge. Provide a wide variety of reading materials and allow students to choose.
- Focus on English vocabulary development using a variety of strategies and materials.
- Model correctly spoken English by restating what a student may have said incorrectly, rather than by overtly correcting the student.

Questions to ask ourselves:
- As a school with a large Hispanic population, have we as faculty members been guilty of blaming demographics for poor performance?
- Have we identified or developed assessment procedures that we can use to measure progress on a weekly or daily basis? How do we use the data to modify our curriculum and instruction or to intervene with specific students?
- Do we stick with a program, rather than choosing a flavor-of-the-month approach?

Resources:
Molineaux, Rebecca. *ERS Focus on Supporting English Language Learners in Mainstream Classrooms*. Arlington, VA: Educational Research Service, 2007.

Nichols, Beverly. *Improving Student Achievement: 50 Research-Based Strategies*. Columbus, OH: Linworth Publishing, Inc., 2008.

Waits, Mary Jo. "Why Some Schools with Latino Children BEAT THE ODDS . . . and Others Don't." 2006. 15 Mar. 2009 <http://www.arizonafuture.org/research/pdf/FAZ502_LatinEd_final.pdf>.

RESEARCH TIP #13
Response to Intervention

The issue:
Response to Intervention is not a new concept, but familiarity with the process and the term has increased exponentially since the 2004 reauthorization of the Individuals with Disabilities Act. Proponents of the concept believe the process can significantly reduce special education rolls, specifically in the area of learning disabilities.

> Scientifically based reading interventions that include phonemic awareness, phonics, fluency, vocabulary and comprehension may be used as part of the process for identifying a learning disability.

The research:
What does Response to Intervention (RTI) entail? The National Association of State Directors of Special Education (NASDSE) includes three components in its definition of RTI: provision of quality instruction and interventions that are differentiated to meet student needs, collection of data over time, and decision making based on the data. The association also states that the intent of RTI is not identification or pre-referral for special education. It is a comprehensive, differentiated system of delivery for curriculum and instruction that requires more than slight modifications to the current processes for meeting learning needs of all students.

Earlier versions of the Individuals with Disabilities Act (IDEA) as well as the 2004 reauthorization contain several provisions relevant to RTI:
- The law requires that before a child is placed in special education, a school must ensure that the child's learning problems are not the result of inadequate instruction.
- The most widely used method of determining learning disabilities is the severe discrepancy method, which compares differences between a student's results on IQ testing and achievement testing. IDEA allows states to use the severe discrepancy method but does not require it.
- The law allows RTI as part of the process in determining if a student has a learning disability.
- The 2004 reauthorization allows schools to use up to 15 percent of special education funds from federal sources on early intervention programs for students not yet identified as in need of special education.
- A specific change in the 2004 reauthorization states that a child cannot be classified as learning disabled if he or she has not had appropriate instruction in reading. Scientifically based reading interventions that include phonemic awareness, phonics, fluency, vocabulary, and comprehension may be used as part of the process for identifying a learning disability.

State departments of education are in the process of providing guidance to school districts within their respective states regarding implementation of RTI. As of January 2008 about 40 percent had finalized regulations, with positions in the proposal stage in most of the remainder. Approaches being used fall into three categories as described by Samuels. Those categories and the number of states using that approach are as follows:
- Permissive, allowing the use of RTI but not requiring it, 37 states

- Transitional, in the process of requiring RTI, four states
- Mandatory, mandating the use of RTI, six states
- No position as yet, three states

The most prevalent model for RTI (though not the only one) is a three-stage model.
- Tier 1: This level focuses on sound curriculum and instruction for all students, with a process for collecting data on individual students as well as student groups as a whole. Interventions in Tier 1 are generally aimed at whole group instructional changes.
- Tier 2: The specific needs of children who do not respond to instruction and whole-group interventions in Tier 1 are addressed. Children receive supplemental instruction that may be determined by problem-solving teams and may include a standard treatment protocol. Students in Tier 2 who demonstrate considerable improvement in foundational academic skills may return to a school's standard instructional program.
- Tier 3: Students who need long-term intervention or who have not responded to Tier 2 interventions move on to Tier 3, which is more intensive but may or may not include referral to Special Education.

Practical implications:
The NASDSE has a framework of core principles for RTI that include the following:
- High expectations: believe that all children can learn.
- Early intervention: address problems at the K-3 level where they can be solved much more easily than problems that are allowed to intensify.
- Data-driven decision making: collect appropriate data regularly and use it to make decisions about individual children.
- Assessments: use assessments appropriate for the functions of screening, diagnosing for particular areas of need, and for monitoring progress.

Questions to ask ourselves:
- What model for RTI has our state established? What specific steps have we as a district taken to review and revise our models for delivery of instruction to meet the needs of all students?
- What assessments do we have in place for diagnosing student needs and monitoring progress?
- What professional development do we as a faculty need to implement our RTI model?

Resources:
Center for Educational Networking. "NASDSE Explains Response to Intervention." *Focus on Results*. 2006. 15 Mar. 2009 <http://new.oakland.k12.mi.us/portals/0/SpecialEd/eLibrary/Evaluation/Focus%20On%20Results%20NASDSE%20RtI%208-06.pdf>.
National Association of State Directors of Special Education. "Myths about Response to Intervention." 2006. 24 Mar. 2008 <http://www.nasdse.org/documents/Myths%20about%20RtI.pdf>.
President's Commission on Special Education. "A New Era: Revitalizing Special Education for Children and Their Families." 2002. 24 Mar. 2008 <http://www.ed.gov/inits/commissionsboards/whspecialeducation/reports/images/Pres_Rep.pdf>.
Samuels, Christina. "'Response to Intervention' Sparks Interest, Questions." *Education Week* (23 Jan. 2008): 1+.

RESEARCH TIP #14
Preschool and Early Childhood

The issue:
According to the National Center for Education Statistics, 74 percent of all children between the ages of three and five are being cared for in nonparental settings. Fifty-seven percent of all children in this age group are in a center-based program, such as a childcare center, a Head Start program, or a preschool/prekindergarten program of some type. What does research tell us about the quality and impact of these programs, especially those with public funding?

> A study of state-funded prekindergarten programs found that children attending these programs showed significant gains regardless of socioeconomic or ethnic backgrounds.

The research:
Longitudinal studies have studied the impact of three specific preschool programs for children in low-income families. These programs are the High/Scope Perry Preschool, the Carolina Abecedarian Project, and the Chicago Child-Parent Centers. Research results have shown the following:
- Students in these programs perform better academically in elementary grades.
- The impact carries over into middle school.
- Fewer children who come out of these programs have been placed in special education or have been retained in a grade.
- Participants have a higher graduation rate and earn more as adults.
- Economists have estimated the economic returns for these programs to be anywhere from four to 16 times as great as the original investment.

What is the extent of state support for preschool education?
- Currently 38 of the 50 states have some provisions for and regulation of preschool programs.
- More than a million children attended a state-funded preschool program in the 2006-07 school year.
- Approximately one-third of the states with provisions for preschool programs provide support for the programs through state school funding formulas. In 2007-08, Oklahoma's funding enabled 70 percent of the state's four-year-olds to be enrolled in a prekindergarten program.

A study of state-funded prekindergarten programs in five states found the following:
- Children attending these programs showed significant gains regardless of socioeconomic or ethnic backgrounds.
- The effect of the prekindergarten programs on children's problem solving abilities and their print awareness was statistically significant. Impact on vocabulary was positive, but not as large.
- Program commonalities across the five states included the following:
  › Nearly all teachers were college graduates with early childhood specialization.
  › Salaries for the preschool teachers were comparable to that of teachers at grades K-12.
  › Class size was 20 students or below, with a teacher's aide in each classroom.

- Because standards for preschool are not as high in all states as in the states in this study, findings cannot be generalized for prekindergarten programs nationwide.

Specific factors have been identified that enable preschool teachers to be more effective. These factors were evident across teacher groups with varying levels of formal education, from fully certified teachers to individuals with no college background.
- More effective preschool teachers received specific training in early literacy and school-readiness skills.
- The teachers were mentored by an experienced colleague.
- Training in the collection and ongoing use of student performance data was provided for teachers.

Practical implications:
Specific components of the three programs included in longitudinal studies can provide guidance for the design of any prekindergarten program. These include the following:
- Be sure to include the children who are most in need, i.e. those children in low-income families or with some other factor that puts them at risk of school failure.
- Hire qualified teachers in sufficient number to maintain a low student-teacher ratio. Provide the teachers with adequate support, including ongoing professional development.
- Use a developmentally appropriate curriculum that gives attention to development of social, motor, and language skills as well as attention to pre-reading skills and number sense.
- Plan and implement a systematic approach to working with parents and other caregivers.
- Conduct ongoing assessment of children's progress through systematic observation. In addition, plan for ongoing evaluation of all components of the program to determine program effectiveness.

Questions to ask ourselves:
- Does the prekindergarten experience we provide for the children we serve address social and physical skills as well as early literacy and mathematics skills?
- What kind of support do we provide for teachers at the preschool level, such as aides, mentoring, and ongoing professional development?
- How can we, as a district, work with childcare centers that serve our preschool population to provide developmentally appropriate, high quality experiences for prekindergarten students?

Resources:
Barnett, W. Steven, et al. "Effects of Five State Prekindergarten Programs on Early Learning." 2007. 18 Aug. 2008 <http://nieer.org/docs/?DocID=129>.

Barnett, W. Steven, et al. *The State of Preschool 2007*. 2007. 18 Aug. 2008 <http://nieer.org/yearbook/>.

Jacobson, Linda. "Support, Data Seen Key to Pre-K Teacher Effectiveness." *Education Week* (10 Oct. 2007): 11.

Schweinhart, Lawrence. "Creating the Best Prekindergartens: Five Ingredients for Long-Term Effects and Returns on Investment." *Education Week* (19 Mar. 2008): 27+.

United States Department of Education, National Center for Education Statistics. "Fast Facts." 2008. 18 Aug. 2008 <http://nces.ed.gov/fastfacts/display.asp?id=4>.

RESEARCH TIP #15
The Gender Gap and Single-Sex Education

The issue:
Differences in the educational status of male and female students have been well documented in data collected over a number of years. Educators continue to develop and implement strategies aimed at meeting the needs of both groups of students. An intervention that has gained increasing attention in recent years is that of single-sex classrooms or schools.

> Boys prefer three quick activities rather than one longer project. Boys like taking tests, girls enjoy writing stories, and both boys and girls like hands-on activities.

The research:
What are some key facts about gender differences in our schools?
- Girls make higher grades in almost every subject, but boys have higher dropout rates, have a higher representation in special education, repeat a grade more often, create more discipline problems, and are more frequently placed in alternative schools.
- Girls generally outperform boys in tests of verbal skills. Achievement differences in mathematics have virtually disappeared between the two sexes.

What does recent research, including brain research, tell us about some of the underlying reasons for these differences?
- Boys are more frequently diagnosed with both attention-deficit disorders and dyslexia. Frustration from these problems may result in boys acting out in class more frequently than girls.
- Girls' hearing is much more sensitive; as a result, they are more distracted by small noises. Boys can function in an actively noisy environment much better than girls.
- The portion of the brain involved in language and handwriting matures about four years earlier for girls than boys; the reverse is true for spatial relations. Best practice is not the same in these instances for boys and girls.

What is the status of single-sex education in the United States?
- American education was initially male-centered but went coeducational in the 1800s. Since that time, single-sex schools have been found primarily in the private sector.
- Title IX legislation passed in 1972 prohibited single-sex classes in most circumstances. Changes in the regulations in 2006 now allow single-sex classes or schools if the same opportunities exist for both sexes and if coeducational classes are also available. Enrollment in single-sex classes or schools must be voluntary.
- The number of single-sex schools and classes is growing rapidly. As an example, in the fall of 2008, 250 schools statewide in South Carolina planned to have single-sex classes, an increase of almost 40 percent from the previous year.

Does the research on single-sex education support this intervention as a valid way to address gender differences?
- Research on single-sex schools in the United States is limited and has been done primarily in private schools.

- Researchers who reviewed studies from several countries concluded there was no evidence for advantages or disadvantages of single-sex classes or schools.
- In a review of 40 studies of the academic achievement in single-sex schools in the United States, analysts found general positive effects favoring single-sex schools over coeducational. However, no long-term benefits have been determined for post secondary measures such as test scores or college graduation rates.
- The same review also found that single-sex education appeared to have a positive effect on educational ambitions, with students taking more rigorous courses and expressing higher aspirations for post-secondary education.
- An Australia study of 270,000 students over a six-year period found that boys in single-sex schools ranked 15-20 percentile points higher than their peers in coed schools.

Practical implications:

Some studies that are in progress indicate attendance is better and discipline problems are fewer. In addition, teachers are learning about the differences in teaching in girl-only or boy-only classes.
- Single-gender girls' classes are easier to teach and move at a faster pace.
- Boys prefer three quick activities rather than one longer project. Boys like taking tests, girls enjoy writing stories, and both boys and girls like hands-on activities.
- Teachers report that both boys and girls participate more in the single-gender classes.
- Staff development is a key component of successful implementation of gender-specific classes.

The research on maturation of different areas of the brain suggests that differentiated instruction needs to address these differences in the primary grades to prevent even bigger differences by middle school.

Questions to ask ourselves:

- Should our school or district consider opportunities for single-sex classes? What issues would we need to address in developing these opportunities?
- Based on available knowledge about the different ways in which boys and girls learn, what changes should we make in our instructional strategies in any classroom—single-sex or coed? What kind of staff development would be beneficial for teachers in our building or district?

Resources:

Clarke, Suzanne. *ERS Focus on Educating Boys*. Arlington, VA: Educational Research Service, 2007.

Clarke, Suzanne. *Single-Sex Schools and Classrooms*. The Informed Educator Series. Arlington, VA: Educational Research Service, 2007.

Corbett, Christianne, Catherine Hill, and Andresse St. Rose. "Where the Girls Are: The Facts about Gender Equity in Education." 2008. 31 July 3008 <http://www.aauw.org/research/WhereGirlsAre.cfm>.

Ferrara, Peter, and Margaret Ferrara. "Single-Gender Classrooms: Lessons from a New York Middle School." *ERS Spectrum* (Summer 2004): 26-32.

Mael, Fred, et. al. "Single-Sex Versus Coeducational Schooling: A Systematic Review." 2005. 31 July 2008 <http://www.ed.gov/rschstat/eval/other/single-sex/single-sex.pdf>.

Sax, Leonard "The Promise and Peril of Single-Sex Public Education." *Education Week* (2 Mar. 2005): 48+.

Section III: School Structure and Organization

RESEARCH TIP #16
Year-Round Schools

The issue:
"Prisoners of Time," the 1994 report of the National Commission on Time and Learning, which is still considered a seminal work dealing with the constraints of time on the American educational system, stated that our schools "have held time constant and let learning vary." Earlier, the 1983 *Nation at Risk* report recommended that districts and states consider seven-hour school days and 200-220 day school years. What is the current status of year-round schools? What does research tell us about their effectiveness?

> Arguments in favor of an extended school year cite international comparisons that show the number of days in United States schools to be considerably less than that of other industrialized nations. For example, Japanese students spend approximately 240 days in school.

The research:
Data from a variety of sources indicate that even though a number of schools operate on a year-round status, there have been few changes since 1983 in the actual amount of time students spend in school:

- Thirty-four states plus the District of Columbia mandate a school year of 180 days or more. Five states require less than 175 days. Most recent data available from the Council of Chief State School Officers show Kansas with the highest requirement at 186 days.
- A traditional school calendar of nine months beginning in late August or early September and ending in late May or early June is the predominant model across the United States.
- Approximately 7 percent of all public schools have changed to a year-round schedule. In the 2006-2007 school year, year-round education programs operated in 46 states, serving more than two million students in 3,000 schools.
- These year-round schedules typically do not add instructional days but spread out the 180 days of schooling across 12 months with shorter vacation breaks.
- Schools have generally adopted year-round schedules for one of two reasons—to alleviate summer learning loss or to deal with overcrowding. Summer learning loss has been well documented and is addressed in detail in Tip #22.
- Almost half of year-round schools create multiple tracks with staggered attendance for different groups on campus at a given time. In some instances, students in multiple-track schools have fewer instructional days than students in the same district who attend on traditional schedules.
- More than half of all year-round schools are in California. Year-round schools are more predominant at the elementary level than the secondary.
- Arguments in favor of an extended school year cite international comparisons that show the number of days in United States schools to be considerably less than that of other industrialized nations. For example, Japanese students spend approximately 240 days in school.
- Arguments against an extended school year are generally twofold. The first is cost. At least one state that initiated legislation to extend the school year reversed its stand because of the high cost involved. The second argument is that more time in school does not automatically translate into more time on task; quality of the time is as important as quantity.

Research studies comparing the impact of year-round schools on academic achievement are limited and often lacking in strong experimental design. Results from some of the studies include the following:
- A meta-analysis of 33 studies found significant positive effects for year-round schools in three-fourths of the studies. Positive results were found for both mathematics and reading.
- A 2000 study in North Carolina of student achievement at the elementary level revealed no significant differences in math or reading between year-round and traditional students.
- A recent doctoral dissertation used Indiana state assessment results for third graders to compare achievement between traditional and year-round schools. Statistically significant differences were found favoring students in year-round schools for the years 2002 through 2005. Differences favoring year-round students were also found for subgroups of students of low socioeconomic status or those designated as special needs students.

Practical implications:
- Year-round schedules appear to help solve the problem of overcrowded schools.
- Strong summer school programs, as described in Tip #23, may be a more realistic way of increasing student achievement and overcoming the summer slide than year-round schedules.

Questions to ask ourselves:
- If we, as a district, are considering a year-round schedule, what is our rationale for doing so? What public relations efforts will be needed to educate our community to the need?
- If we plan to extend the number of days our students spend in school, how will we finance that additional time? How will we ensure that the extra time will actually contribute to improved student achievement?

Resources:
Cooper, Harris. "Summer Learning Loss: The Problem and Some Solutions." 2003. 22 Aug. 2008 <http://www.ldonline.org/article/8057?theme=print>.
Evans, Robert. "A Comparative Study of Student Achievement between Traditional Calendar Schools and Year-Round Schools in Indiana." 2007. 22 Aug. 2008 <http://docs.lib.purdue.edu/dissertations/AAI3287265/>.
Evaluation Services Section, Public Schools of North Carolina. "Year-Round Schools and Achievement in North Carolina." 2000. 21 Aug. 2008 <http://www.ncpublicschools.org/docs/accountability/evaluation/evalbriefs/vol2n2-yr.pdf>.
National Association for Year-Round Education. "Statistical Summaries of Year-Round Education Programs: 2006-2007." Undated. 21 Aug. 2008 <http://www.nayre.org/STATISTICAL%20SUMMARIES%20OF%20YRE%202007.pdf>.
O'Brien, Eileen. "Making Time: What Research Says about Reorganizing School Schedules." 2006. 22 Aug. 2008 <http://www.centerforpubliceducation.org/site/c.kjJXJ5MPIwE/b.2086551/k.9967/Making_time>.
United States Department of Education. "Prisoners of Time." 1994. 21 Aug. 2008 <http://www.ed.gov/pubs/PrisonersOfTime/Prisoners.html>.

RESEARCH TIP #17
Impact of Block Scheduling

The issue:
Block schedules in American schools are not new but have become much more popular during recent years. With the increased call for accountability brought about by No Child Left Behind, some high schools are switching to block schedules as a way to improve student achievement while others are reverting to traditional schedules. Data in current literature indicate that at least 50 percent of high schools in the United States are scheduled around some type of block program. What does current research tell us about the impact of block schedules?

> Academic achievement, as measured by external assessments, does not appear to be dependent on the type of schedule—block or traditional.

The research:
A variety of structures for block schedules exist:
- The 4 X 4 block enrolls students in four classes that meet for approximately 90 minutes every day for a term.
- Alternating A/B day block schedules also have extended class periods, but the classes meet every other day for the entire year.
- The 4 X 4 and the A/B schedules are the most prevalent, but some variations do occur. For example, some schools use the A/B schedule on Monday through Thursday, and then students meet for all classes on Friday.

While some research is now available that compares the different models, research cited here compares the impact of block schedules of any type with that of traditional schedules.

A summary by the Center for Applied Research and Educational Improvement (CAREI) of 20 doctoral dissertations in 12 different states provides the following information:
- Of the 20 studies, 18 compared traditional and block schedules, while two compared different types of block schedules. In the 18 studies that compared traditional and block, nine studies found no differences in academic achievement between students in the two different types of schedules. Results for the other nine studies were fairly evenly distributed across mixed results, results favoring block schedules, and results favoring traditional schedules.
- As noted, some individual studies in the CAREI summary reported mixed findings. A Connecticut study that looked specifically at Advanced Placement courses found no statistically significant differences in any courses except science, where block students outperformed students on traditional schedule. By contrast, however, a University of Virginia study found that college students who had been enrolled in block courses in high school were less successful in college science courses than students from traditional schedules.

Research efforts led by Brian Bottge compared results from traditional and 4 X 4 block schedules: There were no differences in academic achievement:
- Teachers on both schedules used the same kinds of instructional strategies with the time allocated to activities relatively equal.

- Teachers from both groups were satisfied with their schedules.
- Both groups of teachers reported similar interaction with special education teachers, though teachers in the block valued it more.

A research brief from The Principals' Partnership addressed issues other than academic achievement. Benefits cited include the following:
- Schools report fewer discipline problems and fewer failures.
- The time teachers spend on classroom administration is reduced.
- There is more continuity in lessons, with time to engage students in active learning.
- Most schools have the ability to offer a wider variety of courses.
- With a 4 X 4 schedule, students can earn more credits; students who have failed a course have more opportunity to make up the credit and graduate with their class.

Practical implications:
- Academic achievement, as measured by external assessments, does not appear to be dependent on the type of schedule—block or traditional.
- The block schedule does appear to contribute to a more positive school climate.
- While a 4 X 4 schedule may allow students to earn more credits, the schedule can have a negative impact on high stakes assessments. Students who completed a course several weeks earlier than scheduled tests may not have the benefit of timely review.
- Staff development that provides teachers with strategies for how to use extended time effectively is essential when a switch to a block schedule is made.
- Attention to how time is used in the block should not end with the implementation year. Ongoing monitoring of how time is used with additional staff development as needed, for both veteran and newly hired teachers, should be part of any implementation plan.

Questions to ask ourselves:
- If our school is considering a change in structure of the school day, what are the specific goals we expect to accomplish by the change?
- What kind of data do we have that suggests a need for change? What data should we collect to evaluate the success of a change once it is made?
- No matter how our school day is arranged, what are the strategies we have in place to provide the classroom environment and activities that will promote higher student achievement?

Resources:
Bottge, Brian, and John Gugerty. "Block Scheduling: Some Benefits But No Magic Fix." 2004. 12 Aug. 2008 <http://www.wcer.wisc.edu/news/coverStories/block_scheduling.php>.

Bromley, Anne. "Block Scheduling: Not Helping High School Students Perform Better in College Science." *Inside UVA Online* (Spring 2006). 12 Aug. 2008 <http://www.virginia.edu/insideuva/2006/08/block_scheduling.html>.

Center for Applied Research and Educational Improvement. "Research & Resources—Student Achievement." 2006. 12 Aug. 2008 <http://cehd.umn.edu/CAREI/Blockscheduling/Resources/StudentAcheivement.html>.

The Principals' Partnership. "Research Brief: More on Block Schedules." Undated. 12 Aug. 2008 <http://www.principalspartnership.com/blockschedules2.pdf>.

RESEARCH TIP #18
Grade Level Configuration

The issue:
Since the 1990s a number of large city districts, including Cleveland, Cincinnati, Philadelphia, and New York, have begun moving middle grades students into K-8 schools. The beginning of the 2008-2009 school year saw an increased move in this direction in Washington, DC and Baltimore. District administrators claim a large body of research provides evidence that these changes will increase student achievement. Is this actually the case? What does available research tell us about benefits of various grade configurations?

> Research studies have found that transitions between school levels have an impact on learning. Achievement tends to be higher when there are fewer transitions.

The research:
- There are myriad grade configurations in districts across the United States. These include kindergarten-only centers; K-5 and K-6 elementary schools; 5-8, 6-8, and 7-8 middle schools; 7-8 and 7-9 junior highs; ninth-grade only centers; 9-12 and 10-12 high schools; K-8 elementary schools; and K-12 schools. In many cases prekindergarten is added to the mix of configurations.
- The majority of changes that are taking place focus on the middle grades. As noted earlier, many large districts are extending elementary schools to include students through the eighth grade. In other instances the sixth grade is being bounced back and forth between elementary schools and middle schools. In some cases districts are moving to 7-12 schools.
- Much of the research on grade span configuration has been done on rural or middle schools and has not provided any conclusive answers about the best configuration. Studies on student achievement in various configurations tend to be correlational studies based on self-reported data from districts.

Available information from the various research studies includes the following:
- Research studies in Philadelphia have shown that students in K-8 schools outperformed students in middle schools. However, more recent analysis of the findings indicate that more successful K-8 schools were located in higher socioeconomic neighborhoods and had more qualified staff than the middle schools with which they were compared.
- A study of almost 200 schools in Maine found that eighth graders' performance on the state assessment was higher in schools with K-8, K-9, and 3-8 configurations than that of students in middle schools or junior high schools.
- A Pennsylvania study unrelated to the Philadelphia study found benefits for housing sixth graders in elementary schools rather than middle schools. The advantage was greatest for low socioeconomic students.
- A Louisiana study found that students in rural schools or high poverty areas did as well or better in K-12 schools as they in did in separate elementary, middle, and high schools. A Texas study produced similar results.
- There is some evidence from comparing 7-12 and K-8 configurations that middle grade students do better academically in the K-8 setting.

- Some districts have found advantages in single-grade centers, with specific emphasis on ninth grade centers in recent years. After implementing a ninth-grade center, one large California high school has seen improvement on state assessment scores and an increased number of students successfully moving on to tenth grade on schedule.
- Research studies have found that transitions between school levels have an impact on learning. Achievement tends to be higher when there are fewer transitions.
- Transitions also appear to have an impact on student confidence, participation in extracurricular activities, and disciplinary infractions by adolescent boys that result in suspension.

Practical implications:

Other considerations besides improved student achievement have influenced reconfiguration through the years. A 2001 analysis of grade level configuration conducted by the Baltimore City Schools was part of a space utilization study. Regardless of the impetus for considering grade reconfiguration, those who have studied the issue have identified key factors to consider in any changes:

- How far will students have to travel, and what will the cost of that transportation be?
- What impact will there be on parent involvement?
- How appropriate are buildings for the particular age range that will be housed in those buildings?
- How will the interaction between age groups be managed to promote a positive influence of older students on younger ones?
- How will the impact on student achievement be measured?
- How many transitions will students be required to make between school levels?

Questions to ask ourselves:

- How are we dealing with transitions between grade levels in our current grade configuration? What processes and interventions do we have in place to help incoming students be successful academically as well as well-adjusted socially and emotionally?
- If we are considering a change in grade level configurations, what kind of data do we need to collect to inform our decision? What kind of staff development will be needed to prepare teachers for additional curricular and developmental needs?

Resources:

Klump, Jennifer. "What the Research Says (or Doesn't Say) about K-8 Versus Middle School Grade Configurations." 2006. 24 Aug. 2008 <http://www.nwrel.org/nwedu/11-03/research/>.

McEntire, Nancy. "Grade Configuration in K-12 Schools." 2005. 24 Aug. 2008 <http://ceep.crc.uiuc.edu/poptopics/gradeconfig.html>.

Viadero, Debra. "Evidence for Moving to K-8 Model Not Airtight." *Education Week:* (16 Jan. 2008): 1+.

Walker, Karen. "Research Brief: 7-12 Grade Configuration." 2005. 24 Aug. 2008 <http://www.principalspartnership.com/712configuration.pdf>.

Yakimowski, Mary, and Faith Connolly. "An Examination of K-5, 6-8 Versus K-8 Grade Configurations." 2001. 24 Aug. 2008 <http://www.bcps.k12.md.us/Student_Performance/PDF/IR_K5_6_8_Comprehensive_Report_Nov2001.pdf>.

RESEARCH TIP #19
School Size and Small Learning Communities

The issue:
Research that has clearly established the positive impact of smaller schools on student achievement as well as other measures has been a major factor in recent years in the move toward restructuring schools into smaller learning environments. An underlying danger of this movement is that leaders involved in the restructuring process will not consider all the ingredients essential for success. This tip summarizes research prior to the small schools movement as well as more recent research that has identified the components that lead to successful small-school restructuring efforts.

> Small schools report higher rates of attendance and fewer instances of vandalism and classroom disruptions. Differences are especially notable in schools with high concentrations of ethnic minorities and students of low socioeconomic status.

The research:
A 1996 comprehensive study reviewed 31 studies comparing academic achievement of students in large and small schools. A summary of findings included the following:
- Half the studies found no difference in achievement while the other half found that student academic performance was stronger in smaller schools.
- Researchers note that these statistics are correlational, emphasizing that the features of a small school not inherent in larger schools are what produce the actual differences in student achievement.
- Graduation rates are higher in small schools. Students graduating from small schools attend college at a higher rate and are more successful in college than those graduating from larger schools.
- Small schools report higher rates of attendance and fewer instances of truancy, violence, drug and alcohol abuse, vandalism, and classroom disruptions. Differences are especially notable in schools with high concentrations of ethnic minorities and students of low socioeconomic status.
- Students in small schools participate in extracurricular activities at a higher rate than their counterparts in larger schools.
- Large schools do not appear to have the negative effect on achievement of white students that is evident in larger schools serving predominantly poor and minority students.
- One multistate study indicates that small schools reduce the negative impacts of poverty anywhere from 20-70 percent, with the norm being 30-50 percent.
- The impact of school size is evident across all grade levels, but school size tends to be more important at upper grades (especially high school).

A more recent study of smaller learning communities released by the United States Department of Education in 2008 was based on annual self-reported data. Analysis of data resulted in the following conclusions, most of which were consistent with the 1996 study:
- There was no impact on academic achievement as measured by high stakes assessment such as state assessments of college entrance exams.
- A positive trend in the number of students entering a two- or four-year college was evident.
- Ninth graders were more successful in schools with small learning communities. This

was evidenced by more of them moving successfully to tenth grade on schedule.
- Extracurricular involvement increased with organization into small learning communities.

Practical implications:
Many different organizational structures exist in smaller schools, especially at the high school level, but the most prevalent in recent restructuring efforts is Small Learning Communities (SLCs). Several factors have been identified that make SLCs especially effective:
- Both faculty and students have chosen to be in a particular SLC because of a common interest in the focus of that SLC.
- The adult stakeholders in the SLC—faculty, parents, community members—have established a mission and vision that directs all planning and subsequent action.
- The focus is on student learning, with high expectations for all students.
- Learning communities are sufficiently small to enable staff to know the students within the community. Teaching is supported by professional development that is site specific and teacher designed, with built-in time for planning and collaboration.

Barriers to successful implementation have also been identified:
- Insufficient reduction in size is often one of the barriers to successful implementation. Student groups organized as small learning communities may still have too many students to serve in the manner originally envisioned by the SLC movement. Proponents of the movement say that optimal size is 200 students, not the 400 or 500 often found.
- Demands on staff members may be much greater as teachers and administrators seek to become acquainted with and meet individual needs of all students.
- The concept of a comprehensive high school with all that it can offer is hard to break away from. A successful Small Learning Community by design cannot offer students all the activities and academic choices available in a large, comprehensive school.
- Attention to many social aspects of a small learning community may detract from emphasis on academics, inhibiting the desired growth in academic achievement.

Questions to ask ourselves:
- Do we, as a faculty, have a clear vision for the Small Learning Community of which we are currently a member or which we plan to initiate?
- Do we use the structure of the SLC to promote higher student achievement for all students?
- What barriers are keeping us from maximum effectiveness?

Resources:
Chicago Public Schools. "Small Schools Get Results." 2003. 19 Aug. 2007 <http://smallschools.cps.k12.il.us/research.html>.
Cotton, Kathleen. "New Small Learning Communities: Findings from Recent Literature." 2001. 19 Aug. 2008 <http://www3.scasd.org/small_schools/nlsc.pdf>.
Raywid, Mary Anne. "Synthesis of Research/Small Schools: A Reform That Works." *Educational Leadership* (Dec. 1997/Jan. 1998): 34-39.
United States Department of Education. "Implementation Study of Smaller Learning Communities: Final Report." 2008. 19 Aug. 2008 <http://www.ed.gov/rschstat/eval/other/small-communities/highlights.doc>.

RESEARCH TIP #20
Looping

The issue:
Looping is a multiyear placement for students in which a teacher moves with a class of students from one grade level to the next. It is most common at the elementary level but is also used in the middle grades with less frequency. While proponents of looping are enthusiastic about its benefits, quantitative research studies to support benefits are scarce. Most studies are qualitative in nature and focus on affective characteristics rather than academic achievement. What information do these studies provide for us?

> Teachers report that instructional time is gained in the second year of the looping process, because they know what students learned in the previous year. In addition, less time is spent getting to know students and teaching classroom routines.

The research:
Looping is not new. While some would say it originated with the one-room schoolhouse, this is not the case. The one-room schoolhouse consisted of a multiage classroom, where a teacher who stayed at that school for an extended period would—by default—teach the same children over successive grade levels.

- A 1913 memo from the U.S. Department of Education raised the question of whether or not a teacher should move with students and then pointed out advantages of such an arrangement.
- Waldorf Schools have incorporated looping as part of their organizational framework since the first schools were established in 1919.
- Looping is a common practice in some European countries. Some German schools utilize looping for student groups for up to six years.
- Most looping in the United States occurs for a two-year period, i.e. a teacher stays with the same students for two years. However, some schools and districts have implemented a three-year looping cycle.

Rationale for and benefits of looping that are supported by qualitative studies include the following:

- Looping provides stability; this is especially beneficial in situations where students do not have stable home environments.
- Teachers report that instructional time is gained in the second year of the looping process, because they know what students learned in the previous year. In addition, less time is spent getting to know students and teaching classroom routines.
- Insecure students are less apprehensive about beginning the second year with a teacher and classmates they already know.
- English language learners are more comfortable and confident staying with the same teacher.
- Stronger relationships are forged among teachers, parents, and students.

Quantitative studies that address academic benefits have provided the following information:

- A study in Cleveland in the early 1990s found that students in classes that were looped had higher achievement scores than students in traditional classrooms.
- A small study in California reported that students who were in a looping design outperformed their counterparts in regular classes in every area except math concepts

and applications; differences in this study were not calculated using statistical measures.
- A recent study in one school in a large urban California district analyzed sixth grade language arts test results after two years of looping. Results indicated that looped students performed at a statistically higher level in writing, vocabulary, and reading comprehension.

A more extensive Tennessee study that compared performance of elementary students in traditional and looped classes while controlling for initial differences between the two groups found the following:
- Students who had been with the same teacher for two years performed significantly better in both reading and mathematics than students in traditional programs.
- Scores analyzed by gender indicated that girls in a looped program performed significantly better in mathematics at the end of two years than girls in a traditional program. In addition, girls in the looped program outperformed their male counterparts in mathematics at the end of two years, and boys had higher scores in language.

Practical implications:
Some of the problematic areas of looping include the following:
- Conflicts can arise between a student and his teacher or between individual students in the classroom that are difficult to resolve and may not be healthy over an extended period.
- A teacher may have an especially diverse classroom composed of a high number of special needs students; working with such a group for two or more years demands special skills.
- Teachers have to be thoroughly knowledgeable about two or more years of curriculum.
- Schools with high student mobility have difficulty establishing the long-term relationships that are especially beneficial in looping.

Questions to ask ourselves:
- Should we consider looping as an intervention to improve both climate and academic achievement at our school?
- What kind of data should we collect before and during implementation to determine the effectiveness of the program?
- How can we best prepare both staff members and parents for implementation of a looping design? What kind of staff development would be beneficial?

Resources:
Bogart, Vada. "The Effects of Looping on the Academic Achievement of Elementary School Students." 2002. 18 Aug. 2008 <http://etd-submit.etsu.edu/etd/theses/available/etd-0820102-105005/unrestricted/BogartV082302a.pdf>.
Franklin, Cheryl, and Mary Holm. "Looping—How Widespread Is Its Use? Rationale, Evidence Supporting Its Use." Undated. 18 Aug. 2008 <http://education.stateuniversity.com/pages/2194/Looping.html>.
Rodriquez, Carmen, and Bernard Arenz. "The Effects of Looping on Perceived Values and Academic Achievement." *ERS Spectrum* (Summer 2007): 43-55.
Salvetti, Elizabeth. "Looping: Supporting Student Learning through Long-Term Relationships." 1997. 18 Aug. 2008 <http://www.alliance.brown.edu/pubs/ic/looping/looping.pdf>.

Section IV: Intervention Programs

RESEARCH TIP #21
Grade Retention and Social Promotion

The issue:
Grade level retention has been a part of the American public school system since the move from non-graded classrooms to grouping by grades, a move that occurred in the 1860s. Debate about the merits of retention versus social promotion has been ongoing, especially in the last half of the twentieth century and the beginning of this century. Local and state policies enacted in recent years that mandate retention of students whose performance does not meet expectations on high-stakes assessments have intensified the debate. What does research tell us about retention and social promotion? What are the viable alternatives?

> A study of children at several grades found that fear of retention ranked third in a list of anxieties, behind blindness and death of a parent.

The research:
How extensive is grade level retention and what is the impact of the practice?
- The National Association of School Psychologists estimates that 15 percent of all students are held back each year. Approximately one-third of all students have been retained at least one year by ninth grade.
- Retention rates are highest for certain student groups: males, Hispanic or African-American students, those living in poverty, those who change schools frequently, and students with late birthdays.
- A summary of 19 studies conducted during the 1990s indicated that grade retention had a negative effect on achievement in reading, math, and language as well as on social issues such as behavior, school attendance, and peer relationships.
- More recent research has studied the impact of state or district policies that require certain scores on high stakes assessment in order for a student to be promoted. Studies in Chicago found that retained third graders gained no advantage over comparison students who were promoted, and retained sixth graders performed below those students in the comparison group who had been promoted.
- A study of children at several grades found that fear of retention ranked third in a list of anxieties, behind blindness and death of a parent.
- Achievement may increase during the year in which a student is initially held back, but gains fade after two to three years. By then students do no better or perform more poorly than students not retained.
- Retained students are more likely to drop out and are less likely to go on to post-secondary work.
- Retention at both kindergarten and first grade is quite common and surprisingly harmful. Studies indicate that students retained at these grades do not benefit academically and suffer emotionally as a result of being removed from the peer group with whom they had become familiar and comfortable.
- Retention is also common at transition years, i.e. elementary school to middle school and middle school to high school.

Few statistics are kept on the extent of social promotions, partly because districts have not had specific policies related to social promotion.

Opponents of social promotion cite the following disadvantages of the practice:
- Social promotion puts students in grades where they can't do the work; this results in student frustration.
- It increases teachers' work load as they deal with students who have not mastered prerequisite skills.
- Promotion may give parents a false sense of student success; however, some parents have sued for educational malpractice when their students graduate without adequate skills and knowledge.
- Social promotion devalues a high school diploma, especially in the eyes of employers.

Practical implications:

Retention is not cost effective. It means at least one extra year of schooling for each student held back. Early identification of problems and appropriate interventions are less costly and more effective for student achievement. Possible interventions include the following:
- Provide good preschool programs to reduce the large number of students retained at early grades.
- Track individual student progress from early-on using formative and diagnostic assessments; provide timely and appropriate interventions based on assessment data.
- If students are retained, provide for ongoing help beyond the initial retention year.
- Pay special attention to at-risk students during transitions into middle and high school.
- At any level, especially secondary grades, schedule students at risk of failure into classes taught by the best teachers, not the newest or weakest.
- Response to Intervention, addressed in Research Tip #13, provides additional information about early identification and remediation of learning deficiencies.

Questions to ask ourselves:
- What are the preschool options available to all the students in our district? What can we do to enhance the readiness of the children entering our kindergarten classrooms?
- What processes do we have in place to identify and support students at risk of failure at any grade level or in any course?
- Do we provide additional support for those students at transitional grades to help ensure their success at the next level of schooling?

Resources:

David, Jane. "What Research Says about . . ./Grade Retention." *Educational Leadership* (Mar. 2008): 83-84.

Johnson, Deborah. "Critical Issue: Beyond Social Promotion and Retention—Five Strategies to Help Students Succeed." 2001. 12 Aug. 2008 <http://www.ncrel.org/sdrs/areas/issues/students/atrisk/at800.htm>.

National Association of School Psychologists. "Position Statement on Student Grade Retention and Social Promotion." 2003. 12 Aug. 2008 <http://www.nasponline.org/about_nasp/pospaper_graderetent.aspx>.

Owings, William, and Leslie Kaplan. "Standards, Retention, and Social Promotion." *NASSP Bulletin* (Dec. 2001): 57-66.

Thompson, Charles, and Elizabeth Cunningham. "Retention and Social Promotion: Research and Implications for Policy. ERIC Digest Number 161." 2000. 12 Aug. 2008 <http://www.ericdigests.org/2001-3/policy.htm>.

RESEARCH TIP #22
The Summer Slide

The issue:
Research documenting summer learning losses dates back almost 100 years. Summer slide data indicate that achievement scores for the same students tend to be considerably lower in the fall than they were earlier in the spring, just before school dismissed for the summer. Specific information from research about summer loss is the focus of this research tip, while the quality of summer school is addressed in Research Tip #23.

> Because summer reading loss is compounded over years, the cumulative summer losses for low-income students amounts to a two-year achievement gap by middle school.

The research:
Specific research results related to summer learning loss include the following:
- The average achievement loss over summer months is about one month total.
- Losses in mathematics computation are almost three times that large. This may be due to the fact that learning in mathematics usually occurs in the classroom, while reading skills are promoted in a variety of ways outside of school.
- Spelling is another area in which learning loss exceeds the overall average loss of one month.
- Reading comprehension scores for students across all income levels decline across the summer, with greatest losses for students of low socioeconomic status.
- General reading achievement (which includes vocabulary) tends to increase for students from middle-class and affluent families but decreases for students from poor families. The summer decline for students in poor families is about one-third of the gain those students typically make during the school year.
- Because summer reading loss is compounded over years, the cumulative summer losses for low-income students amounts to a two-year achievement gap by middle school.
- One of the strongest predictors of summer reading loss is limited access to books, either at home or at a library.

An extended study of middle-school students in Atlanta conducted more than 30 years ago found the following:
- There is a consistent correlation between the number of books read during the summer and academic gains in the fall.
- Children across all socioeconomic groups who read six or more books showed greater increases in reading achievement than those who read less.
- The library was used by more than half the students in the study. Other research indicates that approximately 10 percent of students attend summer school.

Results from a longitudinal study of 300 Baltimore students conducted by Alexander and colleagues illustrate the impact of the summer learning gap at the elementary level on students at the high school and post-secondary levels. While the researchers include descriptors of factors other than the summer learning decline that influence these outcomes, the correlational data are worth noting.

- The cumulative achievement gains in reading comprehension from first grade through ninth grade reflected learning that took place during the school year.
- The achievement gap at grade nine between students from low and high socioeconomic backgrounds correlated strongly with the difference between those two groups in summer learning at the elementary grades.
- Baseline data at first grade increased with socioeconomic status (SES). The achievement gap between the lowest SES group and the highest, as measured in scale scores, was 26 points.
- School-year gains over a five-year period were slightly higher for students in the lowest SES group than they were for those students in the highest group. Students in the middle SES group made the largest gains during the school year.
- Summer gains and losses were the reverse side of the school-year coin. Over four summers, low SES students regressed in their reading comprehension, middle SES students improved just slightly, and the scale-score improvement of high SES students exceeded that of the other two groups by almost 50 points.
- By grade nine the gap in reading achievement between low and high SES students had increased to 73 points, with all of that difference traceable to the summer differences.
- These achievement differences were reflected in the courses students took at the high school level—non-college track for low SES versus the college prep track for high SES—and the number of high school dropouts versus those students who earned a four-year college degree.

Practical implications:
- The differences in reading achievement at first grade, as indicated in the Alexander study, highlight the need for strong kindergarten and preschool programs, especially in low socioeconomic areas.
- These data have major implications for the quality of summer programs. These quality issues are the focus of the subsequent research tip.

Questions to ask ourselves:
- What kind of program do we have in place to make books easily accessible to students during the summer?
- Have we partnered with our local library to plan or implement such a program?

Resources:
Alexander, Karl, Doris Entwisle, and Linda Olson. "Lasting Consequences of the Summer Learning Gap." 2007. 20 Apr. 2008 <http://www.asanet.org/galleries/default-file/April07ASRFeature.pdf>.

Black, Susan. "What Did You Learn Last Summer?" *American School Board Journal* (Feb. 2005); 38-40.

Boss, Suzie, and Jennifer Railsback. "Summer School Programs: A Look at the Research, Implications for Practice, and Program Sampler." Sept. 2002. 20 Aug. 2008 <http://www.nwrel.org/request/2002sept/summerschool.pdf>.

New York State Education Department. "New York Statewide Summer Reading Program 2008. Research/Promoting Literacy." Apr. 2008. 19 Apr. 2008 <http://www.sharingsuccess.org/code/bv/summerschool.pdf>.

RESEARCH TIP #23
Effective Summer Programs

The issue:
Research documenting summer learning losses was addressed in the previous research tip. More than half the achievement gap between students of lower and higher socioeconomic status can be attributed to unequal opportunities for summer learning. This raises the question of what constitutes an effective summer program.

> Many summer school programs are aimed at students in late elementary or middle school, or high school students making up credits. These interventions may occur too late in students' academic careers.

The research:
Studies dealing with summer school programs provide these findings:
- More than five million American students attend summer school each year; some students go for remediation, while others go for enrichment.
- Both remedial and enrichment programs have been found to have a positive effect on achievement.
- Students at the secondary level take summer classes for a variety of reasons—to raise their grade point average, to take required courses during the summer to allow time for electives during the school year, or to make up courses previously failed.
- There are large variations in time in summer schools across the country, ranging from a low of 15 hours to a high of 315 hours. The average time is 100 hours.
- Research indicates that summer-school programs are more beneficial for long-term learning when they operate for fewer hours a day over an extended number of weeks. A longer schedule reduces the gap between the end of one regular school year and the beginning of another.

Studies of effective summer programs consistently identify five factors that contribute to the success of those programs:
- teacher quality;
- adequate and dependable funding;
- emphasis on reading and mathematics;
- methods that are innovative and creative; and
- a comprehensive plan for program evaluation.

Research specific to teachers within summer programs indicates the following:
- Teachers' knowledge of their students before summer school has been shown to be a strong predictor of students' increase in achievement.
- The quality of interactions between teachers and students is a major distinction between effective and average programs.
- Students have been shown to be more successful in summer programs in which teachers individualize curriculum and instruction rather than using a "one-size-fits-all" approach.
- Remedial programs have more impact when class size is limited; the smaller class size makes individualization much easier.

Summertime data regarding health-related factors are also available:
- Overall, children increase body mass index at nearly twice the rate in summertime as they do during the school year.
- Children who are overweight demonstrate a healthier gain in body mass index during the school year than during the summer.
- According to a 2007 study, only 20 percent of children who received free or reduced meals during the previous school year had access to these meals during the summer.

Practical implications:
- Summer school aimed at remediation requires reteaching of skills not mastered during the regular school year. However, the materials and strategies used during the summer need to approach the instruction in a different way, rather than repeating lessons used during the school year.
- Two ways to add variety are to plan lessons that require physical activity on the part of students and to incorporate learning that is relevant, especially to summertime interests and activities.
- Many summer school programs are aimed at students in late elementary or middle school, or high school students making up credits. These interventions may occur too late in students' academic careers.

Questions to ask ourselves:
- Is the funding for summer school programs adequate and dependable, allowing us to plan well in advance for high-quality programs? Does the funding address teacher compensation and nutritious meals or snacks for participants?
- Are the teachers hired to teach summer school given adequate planning time, with resources that allow them to plan lessons and activities different from those taught during the school year?
- Do we have an evaluation component in place to assess the impact of our program?

Resources:
Center for Summer Learning. "Doesn't Every Child Deserve a Memorable Summer?" Feb. 2008. 19 Apr. 2008 <http://www.summerlearning.org/media/researchandpublications/Memorable.Summer.Fact.Sheet.Final.2.26.08.pdf>.
Center for Summer Learning. "Summertime and Weight Gain." 2007. 20 Apr. 2008 <http://www.summerlearning.org/media/researchandpublications/Summer.Weightgain.Brief.Final.pdf>.
Miller, Beth. "The Learning Season: The Untapped Power of Summer to Advance Student Achievement." 2007. 22 Aug. 2008 <http://www.nmefdn.org/uploads/Learning_Season_ES.pdf>.
Southern Regional Education Board. "Summer School: Unfulfilled Promise." 2002. 19 Apr. 2008 <http://www.sreb.org/programs/srr/pubs/Summer_School.pdf>.
UCLA School Mental Health Project. "Summer and the Living Ain't Easy." June 2003. 19 Apr. 2008 <http://smhp.psych.ucla.edu/atyourschool/june03.htm>.
Walker, Karen. "Research Brief: Summer School." 2004. 19 Apr. 2008 <http://www.principalspartnership.com/summerschool.pdf>.

RESEARCH TIP #24
Effective After-School Programs

The issue:
After-school programs are nothing new but are increasingly more prevalent and popular. Parents of more than 15 million children say their child would participate in an after-school program if it were available within their community. Almost 90 percent of Americans support funding for good after-school programs in low-income neighborhoods. Both the U.S. Senate and House of Representatives have recently formed Afterschool Caucuses. What does current research tell us about the efficacy of such programs?

> After-school programs can be especially beneficial for English language learners (ELLs) in providing additional opportunities to practice their English skills in a nonthreatening environment.

The research:
High-quality research data are scarce. Some studies investigate supplemental programs at different times of the day—before or after school or at lunch time. Researchers at Mid-continent Research for Education and Learning (McREL), in a meta-analysis of available studies, found the following:
- There were small but statistically significant effects on achievement in mathematics and reading.
- The time at which programs were scheduled—before or after school or during the noon hour—did not have a significant influence.
- The programs were more effective at some grade levels than others. The biggest impact in reading was at Grades K-2, while the biggest effect in mathematics was at the high school level.
- The greatest gains resulted from one-on-one tutoring.
- Impact on student achievement was greater for those programs that served students at least 45 hours; however, the effects dropped off considerably when the programs exceeded 100 hours in math or 200 hours in reading.

Researchers for the RAND Corporation, in a review of effectiveness of out-of-school-time programs, reported conclusions similar to those of the McREL team. Their report also identified program components or features that were associated with desired outcomes. These included the following:
- a clearly stated mission that established high expectations;
- an environment that was safe and healthy, both physically and emotionally;
- a stable staff adequately trained to deliver the program and meet the needs of students;
- inclusion of families and the community as partners in the program; and
- ongoing assessment of all aspects of the program.

Research from other sources suggests the following:
- Students who are in the low socioeconomic bracket appear to receive the greatest benefits from after-school programs with an academic orientation.
- Benefits may extend beyond academic ones. Students involved in after-school programs demonstrate less at-risk behavior and have more positive relationships with their peers.
- After-school programs can be especially beneficial for English language learners (ELLs) in providing additional opportunities to practice their English skills in a nonthreatening

environment. In addition, activities in after-school programs often integrate content and activities in a way that helps ELLs make sense of what they are learning.

Practical implications:

A survey of successful after-school programs conducted by the American Association of School Administrators found certain commonalities across those programs. A school or district planning to initiate a new program or retool an existing one can benefit from these conclusions.

- Leaders—superintendent, central office staff, building principals, and after-school staff—are clear about their roles and responsibilities and are committed to the task. Personnel in the after-school programs are well qualified and adequately paid.
- Programs are organized to operate within budget constraints; sustainability is planned for from inception of the program.
- Programs contain both academic and non-academic content, with the academic portions synchronized with what is occurring during the school day.
- Discipline policies in the after-school program are consistent with those under which students operate during the school day.

Common barriers to implementing good after-school programs also exist:

- In some cases expectations are set too low, and the program is not developed and implemented to contribute to academic improvement.
- Roles and responsibilities for personnel involved may not be clearly delineated.
- Bureaucracy gets in the way—both school district policies and regulations and processes for working with external agencies.
- Funding often depends upon external resources; as a result, programs may end when funding is cut.

Questions to ask ourselves:

- What are the goals for our after-school program—whether existing or to be initiated—and how will we measure whether or not we are meeting those goals?
- What procedures can we use to promote a seamless flow between school-day academics and the academics addressed in the after-school program?

Resources:

American Association of School Administrators. "After-School Programs: Bureaucratic Barriers and Strategies for Success." *School Governance and Leadership* (Fall 2005). 31 July 2008 <http://aasa.org/files/PDFs/Publications/SchGovLdrshp/SGLAfterschool.pdf>.

Bodilly, Susan, and Megan Beckett. "Making Out-of-School-Time Matter: Evidence for an Action Agenda." 2005. 31 July 2008 <http://www.rand.org/pubs/research_briefs/2005/RAND_RB9108.pdf>.

Lauer, Patricia, et al. "The Effectiveness of Out-of-School-Time Strategies in Assisting Low-Achieving Students in Reading and Mathematics." 2003. 31 July 2008 <http://www.mcrel.org/PDF/SchoolImprovementReform/5032RR_RSOSTeffectiveness.pdf>.

Shellard, Elizabeth, and Nancy Protheroe. *After-School Programs: A Strategy for Raising Student Achievement.* The Informed Educator Series. Alexandria, VA: Educational Research Service, 2006.

Section V: Technology

RESEARCH TIP #25
Status and Challenges of Technology

The issue:
For the past 10 years a major goal related to technology has been to get more technology into schools. Certainly much more technology of various types is evident, and while student achievement based on use of technology has increased, the improvement is not as great as had been predicted. What is the status of technology in American schools today, and what are some of the challenges we still face?

> Use of computers outside school is outstripping use in school; students often have access to much better hardware and software at home or other locations than at school.

The research:
Access to computers:
- The average ratio of students to computers was 3.8 to 1 in 2006. The variation across states was from a high of five students per computer to a low of less than two.
- Most schools have computer labs and many schools have computers in every classroom.
- At-school access to computers is almost the same for all income levels, ranging between 80 percent and 88 percent.
- Outside of school there is a wide gap, from 37 percent with access at the low socioeconomic end (under $20,000 family income) to 88 percent at the high end ($75,000 or more).

Digital whiteboards are an increasingly popular means for presentation by teachers and for interactive lessons with students. The percent of public schools with digital whiteboards, as reported in "Technology Counts: 2007," is as follows:
- More than 50 percent—8 states
- 36-50 percent—20 states
- 21-35 percent—17 states
- 20 percent or fewer—6 states

Other forms of technology on which data are being collected include hand-held computers, such as graphing calculators in mathematics; laptop loan programs, which are more prevalent in rural schools than in city schools; and streaming video.

State priorities are indicated by attention to technology standards as well as spending priorities. The most recent statistics available regarding technology standards indicate that 32 states have separate technology standards and 16 more have technology standards embedded within core standards. Two states and the District of Columbia have no technology standards, and just four states test students on their knowledge of technology. Data collected from the states indicate the percentage of states that made each of the following areas a major spending priority in 2007:
- Professional development: 53 percent, down from 67 percent in 2006
- Data management systems: 43 percent
- Internet connectivity: 39 percent
- Hardware: 35 percent
- Curriculum, instruction, and assessment: 31 percent

Teachers and administrations have identified specific barriers to the use of technology:
- Computers and technology-based lessons take too much class time to set up.
- Teachers need more training in using the newest technology.
- Teachers need more planning time to create technology-based lessons.
- Access to high-speed computers is inconsistent—many computers are too old to run today's animated and graphic-rich software.
- Districts often do not have enough technical support to resolve problems in a timely manner.
- Use of computers outside school is outstripping use in school; students often have access to much better hardware and software at home or other locations than at school.

Practical implications:
- Districts and individual schools need to have a clear-cut vision for how technology is to be used.
- Technology should always support learning. In the classroom this means the technology used should be aligned with instructional objectives. At the school or district level it may mean that databases have been developed to track student assessment results in order to inform instruction.
- A specific process for evaluating the effectiveness of specific software and other technological tools should be developed in order to maximize use of available funds.

Questions to ask ourselves:
- How does technology specifically support the instructional objectives in each of our classrooms? What steps have we taken to ensure this alignment?
- What kind of ongoing professional development are we providing for administrators and classroom teachers in the use of technology? Does the training take into consideration the varying degrees of proficiency in staff members?
- Have we limited our use of technology to computers, or have we taken advantage of other innovations such as streaming video and interactive whiteboards?

Resources:
Edwards, Virginia (Ed.). "Technology Counts 2006. The Information Edge: Using Data to Accelerate Achievement." *Education Week* (May 4, 2006).

Edwards, Virginia (Ed.). "Technology Counts 2007: A Digital Decade." *Education Week* (Mar. 29, 2007).

Gahala, Jan. "Critical Issue: Promoting Technology Use in Schools." 2001. 16 June 2008 <http://www.ncrel.org/sdrs/areas/issues/methods/technlgy/te200.htm>.

RESEARCH TIP #26
Technology's Impact on Achievement

The issue:
As technology became a major component of the American education scene, an early emphasis was placed on student access to technology through the purchase of hardware. Reauthorization of the Elementary and Secondary Education Act has gone beyond access with the goal of using technology to improve student achievement. State boards of education, as well as legislators, are requiring evidence of the impact of technology on student achievement before committing additional funds.

> Use of technology in low-socioeconomic schools focuses more on remediation, while usage in higher-socioeconomic schools correlates more with higher-order thinking skills.

The research:
Two distinctions in computer use by students can be made. In one case, students learn from computers by using educational software as a tutor or to practice specific skills. Such software includes integrated learning systems and computer-assisted instruction. In the second case, students learn by using technology as a tool or resource to achieve a specific learning goal, to develop higher-order thinking, and to apply research skills. While the first case is the most common one, there is an increasing trend toward use of technology to enhance students' critical thinking and problem solving skills.

Early research focused on computer-assisted instruction. In the last decade, the emphasis has changed. While students still use computers individually to learn content, they are more apt to work as part of a team to develop products related to desired learning goals. Results from research related to this type of usage provide support for ongoing use of computers as an instructional tool.
- One meta-analysis found impact on both the affective and cognitive domains. Teacher-student interaction and student-student interaction were enhanced and problem-solving skills increased.
- A 10-year study in West Virginia looked at the effect of state-wide infusion of technology on assessments based on state standards. Analysis of results indicated that technology use was a major factor in greater-than-expected achievement gains.
- A Missouri study used results on the Missouri Assessment Program to compare performance of students who had been in classrooms supported by Missouri's Instructional Networked Teaching Strategies (eMINTS) with the performance of students whose classrooms had not been in the program. Researchers found that scores in third-grade communication arts and fourth-grade mathematics were higher for eMINTS students; differences were statistically significant for all students as well as students receiving free or reduced lunch.
- A study dealing with the impact of laptop usage indicated that students using laptops write more and their writing is of higher quality, that students using laptops collaborate more with other students, and that teachers who use laptops spend less time lecturing.

Research findings have also resulted in some negative implications.
- Intensive computer usage does not always result in higher achievement. In a correlational study comparing computer use and math scores on the National

Assessment of Educational Progress (NAEP), students who used drill-and-practice software extensively had scores below average while students who used problem solving and application software had scores well above the average NAEP scores.
- Use of technology in low-socioeconomic schools focuses more on remediation, while usage in higher-socioeconomic schools correlates more with higher-order thinking skills.

Practical implications:
What are the right circumstances for classroom computer use that contribute to higher achievement?
- The software being used must be aligned with both the learning objective and the instructional strategies of the teacher.
- Both the knowledge and skills of students and the demands of the software or computer-based assignment must be considered. A good match is needed to maximize student success.
- Staff development for teachers is essential. One study found that students whose teachers had at least 10 hours of training outperformed those whose teachers had five or fewer hours.

Questions to ask ourselves:
- Do my classroom assignments that involve technology support the intended learning goal for that assignment? Do my students have the prerequisite knowledge and skills to be successful?
- Are we using technology to develop higher-order thinking skills as well as research skills, or are we limiting usage to drill-and-practice?

Resources:
Gulek, James, and Hakan Demirtas. "Learning with Technology: The Impact of Laptop Use on Student Achievement." *Journal of Technology, Learning, and Assessment* (Jan. 2005). 03 Mar. 2008 <http://escholarship.bc.edu/cgi/viewcontent.cgi?article=1052&context=jtla>.

Huntley, Lance, and Tracy Greever-Rice. "Analysis of 2005 MAP Results for eMINTS Students." 2007. 03 Mar. 2008 <http://www.emints.org/evaluation/reports/map2005.pdf>.

Lemke, Cheryl. "Why Does Technology Work in Some Schools and Not Others?" Undated. 07 Mar. 2008 <http://www.techlearning.com/techlearning/pdf/events/techforum/sd06/CherylKeynoteHandout.pdf>.

North Central Regional Educational Laboratory. "Critical Issue: Using Technology to Improve Student Achievement." 2005. 16 June 2008 <http://www.ncrel.org/sdrs/areas/issues/methods/technlgy/te800.htm>.

Waxman, Hersh, Meng-Fen Lin, and Georgette Michko. "A Meta-Analysis of the Effectiveness of Teaching and Learning with Technology on Student Outcomes." 2003. 03Mar. 2008 <http://www.ncrel.org/tech/effects2/waxman.pdf>.

RESEARCH TIP #27
Virtual Learning

The issue:
Distance learning is not new, and online learning has raised accessibility to a new level. The vast majority of public colleges and universities offer online courses, and online learning at the precollegiate level has become increasingly popular in the last decade. Recent data indicate that virtual schools are serving almost three-quarters of a million students, mostly at the high school level. What information do available data provide us about the multiple aspects of online learning?

> 58 percent of students surveyed said the quality of online courses was better than the quality of regular classes, while 27 percent rated quality as about the same.

The research:
State departments of education and state legislatures have assumed the oversight of virtual learning in numerous states.

- There are 24 states with state-led online education programs and 26 states with state policies to regulate online programs. Of these states, 12 have both programs and policies. Another 12 states have neither state-led programs nor policies to regulate programs within the state.
- Organizational models of state-led programs vary. The programs may function under the auspices of a state or local educational agency, as an independent entity, as a separate school district, or be housed at a university.
- Almost all states require that online courses meet state academic-content standards, but there have been some problems in ensuring that full-time online students take state tests.
- Michigan has a law mandating that high school students take part in an online learning experience to graduate.
- The summary of state processes and regulations compiled by John Watson cites Kansas as having perhaps the best system in the country for tracking online programs. Specific information about the system as well as sources for additional information are provided in Watson's report.

While many people tend to think of online learning in terms of the complete education of students involved, this is not the case. For the majority of online students, the courses are supplemental to the education venue in which they spend most of their time. A survey completed by students at Florida Virtual High School, one of the oldest virtual schools in the country, provided a wealth of information about the students' viewpoint of online learning.

Their reasons for taking online courses:
- To take an extra course, including ones not available at their home high school.
- To balance academic and extra-curricular demands and alleviate conflicts between the two.
- To make up a course in which an unsatisfactory grade had been earned.

Their analysis of course difficulty and quality:
- 39 percent of students said virtual courses are harder or much harder than regular face-to-face courses; they cited the absence of teachers to help.
- 23 percent said courses are easier, while 29 percent rated courses at the same level of difficulty.
- 58 percent of students surveyed said the quality of online courses was better than the quality of regular classes, while 27 percent rated quality as about the same.

What do students cite as advantages and disadvantages of virtual learning?
- Learning is not time bound; it can be done at home, at anytime of the day or night.
- Students can proceed at their own rate.
- Communication with teachers is good, but communication with other students is poor.
- Distractions from other students are not a problem, but distractions at home can be.
- Students also recognized that, to be successful in online learning, a student needs to be an independent learner. Florida Virtual High School had to establish specific timelines, which they classified as accelerated, regular, and extended.

And, finally, what about student achievement in virtual classrooms?
- Students' performance in virtual classrooms has been found to be as good as or better than their performance in face-to-face classrooms. Achievement gains are stronger in Web-based programs that include an email component between teacher and students.

Practical implications:
- Voluntary standards for instructors in virtual classrooms have been developed. One standard suggests that teachers in virtual classrooms should complete an online course before assuming the responsibility of teaching one.

Questions to ask ourselves:
- What kind of virtual learning opportunities do the students in our school or district have? How do we evaluate the quality of these opportunities, including ones that we offer ourselves?
- What kind of counseling is in place to assist students in making appropriate decisions about enrolling in virtual classes?

Resources:
Edwards, Virginia (Ed.). "Technology Counts 2002. E-Defining Education." *Education Week* (May 9, 2002).

Edwards, Virginia (Ed.). "Technology Counts 2007: A Digital Decade." *Education Week* (Mar. 29, 2007).

Tucker, Bill. "Laboratories of Reform: Virtual High Schools and Innovation in Public Education." 2007. 19 June 2008 <http://www.educationsector.org/usr_doc/Virtual_Schools.pdf>.

Watson, John, and Jennifer Ryan. "Keeping Pace with K-12 Online Learning." 2006. 19 June 2008 <http://www.nacol.org/docs/Keeping%20Pace%20with%20K-12%20Online%20Learning%202006.pdf>.

Section VI: Brain-Based Learning

RESEARCH TIP #28
The Brain and Attention

The issue:
Knowledge about the brain and how it works has grown exponentially in the last century, especially in the last quarter century. Focus for educators has moved from the right-brain/left-brain application of the 1970s to a more biological understanding of the entire brain. While much brain research cannot be directly translated into classroom practice, there is still a wealth of information that *can* guide our decisions.

> Emotion is one of the things that makes the brain pay attention, and emotion is especially pertinent at the middle school level. Emotions can be invoked through use of humor, projects, and hands-on activities.

The research:
Attention, the ability of an individual to concentrate or focus on an object or a thought, is an ever-present concern for educators. Recent brain research related to attention includes these findings:
- Sprenger (2005) describes five types of attention: sustained attention, which requires focus for a longer period of time; directed attention, which responds to a particular stimulus; selective attention, a specific choice by an individual; divided attention, when focus changes rapidly from one stimulus to another; and focused attention, when attention is directed to a particular stimulus for a specific reason.
- Focused attention is a prerequisite for successful direct instruction. The length of time for which direct instruction is effective can be as low as five minutes at kindergarten and increases to about 15 minutes by senior high.
- Change makes the brain pay attention.
- Events and activities that provide contrast or novelty help students focus their attention.
- The brain has natural attention highs and lows that run in 90-110 minute cycles. Attention spans in the daytime relate to these highs and lows just as light and deep sleep follow the cycles at night.
- The brain is more efficient in processing information during a natural high.
- Brain chemicals greatly influence students' attention at school.
- Acetylcholine is a chemical associated with drowsiness; it is usually present in higher amounts in the late afternoon and evening.
- The brain consists of about 80 percent water. Drinking lots of fluid helps to keep the brain alert and focused.

Practical implications:
- Attention can be primed. Students are more apt to attend to something when they have specifically been instructed to do so.
- Emotion is one of the things that makes the brain pay attention, and emotion is especially pertinent at the middle school level. Emotions can be invoked through use of humor, projects, and hands-on activities.
- Class work that is relevant and active is more apt to hold attention than work that is irrelevant and passive. Use strategies that are personal, and incorporate physical involvement when feasible.

- Avoid or use sparingly activities that are out of context and have little interaction, such as extensive lecture or seatwork.
- Various kinds of stimuli attract attention initially. However, if a particular stimulus is ongoing it tends to be ignored after time and loses its effectiveness.
- Choices are more effective than requirements in keeping attention. Whenever possible, provide choices related to assignments, projects, resources, and cooperative work with classmates.
- Vary activities to allow processing after new learning. Meaning is generated internally and needs time to solidify.
- The time needed for processing depends on the type of learning. New content with lots of "meat" requires longer and more frequent processing periods than review of familiar material.
- Time spent in mastering required skills can reduce active attention and sometimes defeat the intended outcome unless a variety of strategies are used for practicing the skills.
- Use novelty to focus attention, but balance it with routine. The predictability of routine contributes to a low-stress environment, while novelty captures attention.
- Novelty need not be flamboyant. It can be a change of location (by the teacher or the class), a variation in presentation styles (such as group work or projects), or a different presenter.
- Provide students with mental breaks or the opportunity to move about for a brief period to alleviate drowsiness.

Questions to ask ourselves:
- What routines are currently observed (in your classroom or in the school as a whole) that promote learning but provide a low-stress environment?
- Think of a lesson you taught during the last week in which the attention span you expected was too long. How could you restructure that lesson to maximize student attention and learning?

Resources:
California Department of Education. "Adolescent Development and Instruction, Assessment, and Intervention." Undated. 27 Aug. 2008 <http://pubs.cde.ca.gov/tcsii/ch2/adlescntdevchpt2.aspx>.

Jensen, Eric. *Teaching with the Brain in Mind*. Alexandria, VA: Association for Supervision and Curriculum Development, 2005.

Sprenger, Marilee. *How to Teach so Students Remember*. Alexandria, VA: Association for Supervision and Curriculum Development, 2005.

Sprenger, Marilee. *Learning & Memory: The Brain in Action*. Alexandra. VA: Association for Supervision and Curriculum Development, 1999.

Sylwester, Robert. *A Celebration of Neurons*. Alexandria, VA: Association for Supervision and Curriculum Development, 1995.

RESEARCH TIP #29
The Brain and Memory

The issue:
Because memory provides both the basis for learning and the evidence of any learning that has taken place, educators continually look for ways to enhance memory capacity. Recent brain discoveries related to memory, both the types of memory and the retrieval of material stored in memory, have important classroom implications.

> Organizing information in meaningful chunks or relationships increases ability to remember and recall the information.

The research:
Brain research related to memory includes these findings:
- Memories are located in many places in the human brain, with location dependent on memory type.
- Memory retrieval as a process is more important than location. Retrieval is most successful when conditions for retrieval match conditions for learning.
- Explicit memory can be semantic (factual, linguistic, memorized) or episodic (related to location, event, or context).
- Most classroom instruction is geared to semantic memory, which requires frequent repetition for learning to occur. Semantic memory can process limited amounts of information for short periods of time and has the weakest retrieval system.
- Episodic memories are more easily internalized because they are linked to a context, location, or event. Efficient retrieval depends on a similar context.
- Thematic instruction provides a context that allows students to utilize episodic memory in learning facts, skills, and concepts from various disciplines. Learning may be doubled in a thematic unit.
- Implicit memory can be procedural (requiring both mental and physical processing) or automatic (reflexive). Some content that is originally semantic, such as math facts, may become automatic.
- Procedural learning involving hands-on activities is easier to master than semantic, requires less review, and leaves more positive memories.
- Organizing information in meaningful chunks or relationships increases ability to remember and recall the information.
- Visualization, even for students who are not primarily visual learners, assists students in committing new material to memory.
- Emotion can serve either a positive or negative role in remembering. Students who are anxious or depressed are not receptive to remembering what they have just heard or read. Brain research has shown, however, that positive emotions have a powerful influence on what will be remembered.
- Processing time is required for new learning to solidify and be retained. The amount of processing time depends upon whether the material is brand new with lots of content or review material to which students have had previous exposure. The new material may require extended processing time, while review material takes much less time.
- Summarizing, comparing, and contrasting are ways in which students can process information.

- Knowledge moves from short-term to long-term memory through repeated practice over time.
- Sleep can be a major factor in remembering new learning. Research indicates that cutting back on sleep can reduce the brain's ability to store and hold new material.

Practical implications:
- Plan instruction to incorporate appropriate physical activity whenever possible.
- Use graphic organizers to help students chunk semantic information for processing and commitment to memory.
- Allow processing time or practice—immediate and over time—so that learning is transferred to long-term memory.
- Provide options for processing that meet students' individual needs and learning styles.
- Incorporate thematic teaching to provide meaningful context that enhances memory and learning.
- Create positive emotional experiences through music, drama, group interaction, or class celebrations.
- Match assessment (memory retrieval) to instructional method and location. Students will not do as well on a mathematics test administered in an English classroom as they will when the same test is given in the room in which they learned the material.
- Cramming may produce short-term gains but does not contribute to long-term retention of knowledge.

Questions to ask ourselves:
- What opportunities for processing do I provide my students after presenting new material?
- Are my practice and review sessions distributed over time so that students can move learning from short-term to long-term memory? Do I use a variety of activities for practice and review to meet the different learning styles in my classroom?
- Does my classroom environment contribute to a positive emotional experience?
- Are the memory retrieval systems called for in my assessments compatible with the context in which my students learned the material?

Resources:
Caine, Renate, and Geoffrey Caine. *Teaching and the Human Brain*. Alexandria, VA: Association for Supervision and Curriculum Development, 1994.

Jensen, Eric. *Teaching with the Brain in Mind*. Alexandria, VA: Association for Supervision and Curriculum Development, 2005.

Sprenger, Marilee. *How to Teach so Students Remember*. Alexandria, VA: Association for Supervision and Curriculum Development, 2005.

Sprenger, Marilee. *Learning & Memory: The Brain in Action*. Alexandria, VA: Association for Supervision and Curriculum Development, 1999.

RESEARCH TIP #30
More Strategies for Brain-Based Learning

The issue:
The previous two tips focused on attention and memory, two specific topics of major importance in the interaction between teaching and learning. In the past quarter century volumes have been written describing the physiological aspects of the brain, the myriad ways in which learning takes place, and recommendations on how educators can apply these findings. This tip includes a selection of those recommendations.

> Students learn and comprehend more when the senses and physical movement are involved along with the brain.

The research:
Renate and Geoffrey Caine have synthesized brain research into 12 principles for educators. The implications of those principles for teaching and learning are paraphrased here. Some of the implications reinforce information included in Tips #15, #28 and #29.

- Students learn and comprehend more when the senses and physical movement are involved along with the brain.
- Teaching is more effective when students have the opportunity for social relationships and interactions.
- Children have the capacity to learn more when their specific interests and needs are being met by what is being taught.
- Students learn best when they can create new patterns and link them to ones already formulated.
- Teachers can increase learning by effectively using emotions during instruction.
- Effective instruction embeds details into the big picture.
- The context in which specific ideas and concepts are presented can enhance student learning of the material.
- Students should be allowed time to reflect on or process the information they have received.
- Students learn best from learning activities that utilize both rote memory of facts and skills and dynamic memory that is actively involved in reacting to everyday experiences.
- Instruction should take into account individual differences in development and prior knowledge.
- Classroom environments should be supportive and nonthreatening.
- Students comprehend more when their specific interests and abilities are engaged.

These principles are illustrated in some of the practical implications that follow.

Practical implications:
Motivation is related to increased levels of specific chemicals in the brain. Jensen (2005) describes specific steps that teachers can take to encourage the release of these chemicals. Some of these strategies have been described elsewhere, but not in relation to motivation.

- Reduce threats by finding out what inhibits learning and what makes learning more enjoyable for students in the classroom.
- Develop a climate that focuses on the positive aspects of learning and encourages student self-efficacy.

- Use emotions productively through development of class rituals or traditions; use of music, art, and drama; celebrations of success, for individuals or the class as a whole; and through the satisfaction of some type of service to others.
- Encourage students to set goals, sometimes on a daily basis. Goal-setting may be a logical act, but emotions enable an individual to accomplish the goal.
- Provide feedback on an ongoing basis, including ways that students can identify their own progress through methods such as rubrics or peer editing.

More than 30 years of research has confirmed that experiences in life change the brain, sometimes for the good, but sometimes in a negative way.
- Young brains have areas that are not committed to any function and synapses that are not yet in use.
- Appropriate experiences, especially those aimed at enrichment, can help these brains develop in a positive way.
- An enriched environment stimulates all the senses, but not necessarily at the same time. Stimulating different senses contributes to growth in different areas of the brain.
- Two factors that support positive brain development are physical activity and good nutrition. (See Tips #35 and #36 for the impact these two factors have on achievement.) While schools have some control over both of these, a school-based program to educate parents about both would have potentially greater impact.
- Jensen (2006) defines enrichment as "conditions for positive contrast" rather than a single activity aimed at an entire classroom.
- To create conditions for contrast it is essential that a teacher know and understand his or her students to determine how these conditions can be manipulated at various times and for different individuals or subgroups within the classroom.
- Providing students with a choice of activities that support the learning objective or planning a tiered activity that allows students to enter at an appropriate level are ways in which conditions for contrast can be established.

Questions to ask ourselves:
- What kind of program do we have in place as a school to educate parents about the importance of good nutrition and physical activity? As a school, are we implementing what we know about those factors in order to enhance both brain development and student achievement?
- How am I creating "conditions for positive contrast" in my classroom? Do I know enough about all of the students in my class to provide contrast (differentiation) for each one of them?

Resources:
Caine, Renate, and Geoffrey Caine. "Overview of the Systems Principles of Natural Learning." Undated. 28 Aug. 2008 <http://cainelearning.com/files/Summary.pdf>.
Diamond, Marian. "What Are the Determinants of Children's Academic Successes and Difficulties?" 1999. 28 Aug. 2008 <http://www.newhorizons.org/neuro/diamond_determinants.htm>.
Jensen, Eric. *Enriching the Brain: How to Maximize Every Learner's Potential*. San Francisco, CA: Jossey-Bass, 2006.
Jensen, Eric. *Teaching with the Brain in Mind*. Alexandria, VA: Association for Supervision and Curriculum Development, 2005.

Section VII: Advanced Placement

RESEARCH TIP #31
Advanced Placement and Student Achievement

The issue:
The Advanced Placement (AP) Program was initiated in 1955. The College Board describes it as "a collaboration between motivated students, dedicated teachers, and committed high schools, colleges, and universities." What does this collaboration entail? What does an AP program look like? Is there evidence to indicate that completing AP courses makes a difference in academic achievement?

> Several research studies have indicated that an AP exam grade of three or higher is a strong predictor of a student's ability to complete college and earn a bachelor's degree.

The research:
Specific facts about the Advanced Placement Program include the following:
- In 2007, 37 courses were available in a variety of subject areas. This number was reduced by four in the 2009-2010 school year.
- The average number of courses available to students in individual schools is nine. Numbers are higher at many schools and lower at others.
- While faculty members at each school have control over their curricula and are responsible for developing their own syllabi, the College Board provides each AP teacher with a set of expectations, which have been established by university personnel for college-level courses.
- AP exams are developed with the intent to create assessments of college-level learning.
- Most colleges and universities in the United States as well as 30 other countries use AP-exam results for awarding of college credits or for placements of students in higher-level courses.
- Composite scores on AP exams are converted to a scale of one through five. The College Board defines success on an AP exam as a score of three or higher. A score of three is considered to be equivalent to mid-level B to mid-level C work in college. A score of four corresponds to a strong B or low A, while a score of five generally correlates to high-level A work in the corresponding college course.
- Students from more than 15,000 schools in the United States took just under two million AP exams in 2007.
- The percentage of students who took an AP exam at some time in high school increased from 18 percent in 2002 to almost 25 percent in 2007.
- The proportion of students who earned a three or higher on an AP exam during high school was 15.2 percent of the entire U.S. high school population in 2007, an increase of 4.5 percent over 2002.
- The five top AP exams by number taken in 2007 were U.S. History, English Literature and Composition, English Language and Composition, Calculus AB, and U.S. Government and Politics.

Does enrollment in AP courses or completion of an AP exam make a difference in college performance? Mixed research results include the following:
- Several research studies have indicated that an AP exam grade of three or higher is a strong predictor of a student's ability to complete college and earn a bachelor's degree.
- A Texas research study found that students who were able to bypass introductory college courses because of success on AP exams earned higher grade point averages (GPA) in college and took more credit hours in the subject area of their exam than non-AP students with similar high school ranks and SAT scores.
- Another Texas study used SAT scores and socioeconomic status as control variables to analyze the impact of AP course taking with no exam and AP course taking followed by completion of the appropriate exam. Students who took the AP course but not the exam had higher college GPAs than non-AP students, and GPAs for students who completed both the course and the exam were higher yet.
- In contrast, a California study found that completion of honors and AP courses in high school bore little relationship to a student's performance at the university level.
- Researchers at two major universities found that an AP exam score of five did not guarantee that a student would earn an A in the same course in college.
- The Third International Math and Science Study found that U.S. students in advanced math and science courses fared poorly in comparison with students in other countries. The exception was in Advanced Placement courses, where even students who scored a one or two on calculus and physics exams ranked at the top or very close to the top of all scores from other nations.
- Anecdotal evidence suggests that students who score a one or a two on an AP exam are more successful in college than if they had not taken the exam. However, there is no research evidence to support this.

Practical implications:
- Some states are giving more focused attention to the creation and implementation of a vertically articulated 6-12 curriculum that will prepare students for AP courses.
- Efforts are being made to expand availability of AP courses to rural students; virtual learning is one medium being used.

Questions to ask ourselves:
- What kind of data do we collect and analyze on our AP students and their subsequent success in college?
- Do the courses we offer for students at our school meet students' needs and interests? Are our offerings adequate, or should they be expanded?
- Does vertical articulation across Pre-AP and AP courses in our school provide students with the opportunity to be successful in culminating AP courses?

Resources:
College Board. "Advanced Placement Report to the Nation." 2007. 29 July 2008 <http://www.collegeboard.com/prod_downloads/about/news_info/ap/2007/2007_ap-report-nation.pdf>.
College Board. "The 4th Annual AP Report to the Nation." 2008. 29 July 2008 <http://professionals.collegeboard.com/profdownload/ap-report-to-the-nation-2008.pdf>.

RESEARCH TIP #32
Challenges of Advanced Placement Implementation

The issue:
The popularity of Advanced Placement (AP) programs has grown immensely. More than 130,000 teachers at more than 14,000 high schools teach AP courses. The College Board offers twice as many tests as it did 10 years ago, and the number of students taking AP exams has increased rapidly in the past several years. What are some of the challenges that have been created by this growth?

> African-American and Hispanic students are generally underrepresented in AP enrollment. Discrepancies for Hispanic students are largest in those states with large Hispanic populations.

The research:
Not all universities routinely give credit or place students in advanced courses as a result of AP exams. Some major universities require many students to take introductory courses, even if those students have passed AP exams in those courses. Other universities are reviewing AP policies because of concerns that students are being advanced without acquiring skills necessary for success in later courses. These concerns led to the first-ever audit of AP courses.

- The AP audit was initiated by the College Board in 2005 to address concerns that quality of AP programs was declining as popularity increased.
- The goal of the audit was to ensure up-to-date courses with the desired rigor. Schools were required to submit syllabi of AP courses for review of college faculty.
- Two-thirds of the syllabi submitted were approved on initial review. The remainder were returned for revisions, and the majority of those were revised and resubmitted.
- The number of schools offering at least one AP course dropped 13 percent in the 2007-08 school year after the audit of AP courses was initiated. Data were not available to indicate if this was the result of courses that were not approved or if some schools simply chose not to submit syllabi.
- Scores for all students have declined over recent years.
- As noted earlier, the number of AP exams taken increased by almost 25 percent over a four-year period. In the same timeframe, the percent of students earning a satisfactory score (three or higher) decreased from just under 60 percent to 57 percent.
- The average score of 2.83 for all students in 2007 was also lower than the average score of 2.9 in 2003. A decline in the average score was evident for all ethnic groups except Asian Americans.
- Statisticians attribute the decline in scores to the increased number of test takers, but educators and policy makers who are seeking to increase access for all students also want to maintain high quality and high levels of performance.
- Discrepancies are apparent in access to courses as well as performance on exams across various ethnic groups.
- African-American and Hispanic students are generally underrepresented in AP enrollment.

Discrepancies for Hispanic students are largest in those states with large Hispanic populations.
- The same pattern occurs for African-American students when the percentage of AP test takers is compared with the proportion of African-American students in the overall

population. However, the representation of Hispanic students among AP test takers is very similar to the proportion of Hispanic students in the overall population.
• The average score for 2007 exams across all students was 2.83. Scores for major ethnic groups were 3.05 for Asian students, 2.95 for white, 2.39 for Hispanic students, and 1.91 for African-American students.

Practical implications:
Personnel at the College Board as well as policy makers at federal and state levels have taken specific steps to address some of these issues.
- Several states have passed legislation that expands access to AP courses. Arkansas, for example, has a law that requires all public schools in the state to make AP courses available to their students. Mississippi has the same requirement but also requires AP teacher training.
- Teacher participation in AP and Pre-AP professional development programs has been increased as a result of higher levels of state funding.
- More attention has been given to the vertical articulation of Pre-AP and AP courses in grades 6-12 so students come to AP courses better prepared for the rigors of those courses.
- The Advanced Placement Incentive Program (APIP) is a federally funded program that provides grants to both state and local education agencies. The purpose of the program is to increase enrollment of low-income students in Pre-AP and AP courses and to increase the number of low-income AP test takers.
- Additional initiatives from the College Board are aimed at increasing AP participation of low-income and minority students and providing grants for teachers of those students to attend AP Institutes.

Questions to ask ourselves:
- What steps have we taken to ensure that rigor in our AP courses is maintained while we promote higher participation in those courses?
- Have we analyzed the enrollment of minority students in our courses and compared those enrollments with student body demographics? What steps are we taking to eliminate gaps?
- What kind of professional development are we providing for teachers in AP and Pre-AP courses?

Resources:
Cech, Scott. "AP Trends: Tests Soar, Scores Slip." *Education Week* (20 Feb. 2008): 1+.
Cech, Scott. "College Board Intends to Drop AP Programs in Four Subjects." *Education Week* (9 Apr. 2008): 13.
College Board. "Advanced Placement Report to the Nation." 2007. 29 July 2008 <http://www.collegeboard.com/prod_downloads/about/news_info/ap/2007/2007_ap-report-nation.pdf>.
College Board. "The 4th Annual AP Report to the Nation." 2008. 29 July 2008 <http://professionals.collegeboard.com/profdownload/ap-report-to-the-nation-2008.pdf>.

Section VIII: Special Certification Status

RESEARCH TIP #33
The Impact of Alternative Certification

The issue:
The original enactment of No Child Left Behind legislation included a requirement that all classrooms be staffed with "highly qualified" teachers by the end of the 2005-06 school year. By NCLB definition, highly qualified teachers will hold at least a bachelor's degree, have full state teacher certification or hold a license to teach after passing the state licensure exam, and demonstrate competence in each academic subject in which they teach. Under NCLB definitions, there are a variety of ways in which teachers may demonstrate competence. What do current data tell us about the extent of alternative certification and its impact on student achievement?

> Teachers who come to teaching through alternative routes demonstrate greater concern about delivering effective instruction, especially in the area of planning lessons.

The research:
What is the history of alternative certification?
- There are more than three million teachers in the United States. Teacher-education programs at colleges and universities produce about 90 percent of those teachers.
- Alternative certification programs produce the rest, bringing almost 200,000 teachers into the profession every year.
- Alternative certification has been practiced informally for a number of years. The concept was formalized in New Jersey in the mid 1980s and has been accepted in policy and practice in almost all states.
- Support for alternative routes to certification has grown because of supply-and-demand issues. Student population has increased, many teachers are retiring while others leave the field shortly after entering it, and legislation reducing class size has been passed in many states.
- Most individuals who enter the profession through alternative certification routes are adults who enter education as a second profession.
- One advantage of alternative certification is the opportunity to bring individuals into the profession who have a broad range of experience as well as a desire to make a difference in students' lives. A second advantage is the opportunity to employ bright college graduates who majored in a content area rather than pursuing a teacher education program.
- Almost 500 alternative certificate programs are in operation across the country. Many of these programs are operated by the same colleges and universities that provide traditional programs and may look very similar.

Mixed results are apparent in research studies that compare the quality of teachers who come through a traditional preparation program with those who receive alternative certification.
- The U.S. Department of Education has stated that there is no evidence that education coursework contributes to teacher quality. However, other research indicates that teachers who come through alternative certification feel less prepared than those who complete traditional programs.

- Research indicates that a teacher's sense of efficacy has a direct impact on teacher quality and, as a result, makes a difference in student achievement. Surveys of teachers entering the profession have found that teachers who enter via alternative certification have lower levels of efficacy than those beginning teachers who complete a traditional program.
- Teach for America (TFA) is one of the more widely known alternative certification programs. Several recent studies have compared academic performance of elementary and middle school students with TFA instructors with the performance of students with traditionally prepared teachers. Students in TFA classrooms were found to outperform their peers in non-TFA classrooms in mathematics, but not in reading.
- A North Carolina study focused on TFA teachers in high school classrooms. Results in student performance favored those students who were taught by TFA corps members, with especially strong results in mathematics and science.

Practical implications:
- Surveys indicate that just half of the alternative certification beginners felt prepared for their first year, compared with 80 percent of the traditionally prepared beginners.
- Teachers who come to teaching through alternative routes demonstrate greater concern about delivering effective instruction, especially in the area of planning lessons.
- Actual classroom experiences are limited in alternative certification programs. More than half the teachers in these programs indicated they could have benefited from more time with a classroom teacher; almost one-fifth of the teachers said they had spent no time with a teacher before assuming their first job.
- Numerous studies cite the placement of teachers from alternative certification programs in high needs schools.

Questions to ask ourselves:
- What kind of mentoring and support do we have in place for beginning teachers? Are the specific needs of individuals with alternative certification considered?
- As a district, what kind of policies do we have about assignment of new teachers? Do we routinely assign them to the most difficult situations? What changes should we make?

Resources:
Forsbach-Rothman, Terry, Marcia Margolin, and Diane Bloom. "Student Teachers and Alternate Route Teachers' Sense of Efficacy and Views of Teacher Preparation." 2007. 15 Mar. 2009 <http://www.alt-teachercert.org/JNAAC/JNAAC_Spring_2007.pdf>.
Honawar, Vaishali. "Reports Renew Debate over Alternative Preparation." *Education Week* (19 Dec. 2007): 11.
Sawyer, Gayle, and Belinda Gimbert. "Policies and Practices for Selecting Highly Effective Teachers for Alternative Certification Programs." 2008. 30 July 2008 <http://www.alt-teachercert.org/NAAC_Online_Journal_Spring_08_Issue.pdf>.
Starzyk, Edith, and Scott Stephens. "More Often, Path to Classroom Is an Indirect Route." 2008. 30 July 2008 <http://www.innovations.harvard.edu/news/100391.html>.
Xu, Zeyu, Jane Hannaway, and Colin Taylor. "Making a Difference?" The Effects of Teach for America in High School." 2007. 30 July 2008 <http://www.urban.org/UploadedPDF/411642_Teach_America.pdf>.

RESEARCH TIP #34
Board-Certified Teachers and Student Achievement

The issue:
In December of 2007 an article in the *Chicago Sun-Times* reported that more than 200 Chicago Public Schools were certified by the National Board of Professional Teaching Standards (NBPTS) in 2007. That put the district well on the way to Mayor Richard Daley's goal of 1,200 Board-certified teachers by the end of 2008. In the article the mayor was quoted as saying that "National Board-certified teachers have a huge impact on their students and are a tremendous asset to our school system." What is the status of Board-certified teachers nationwide, and do those teachers have a greater impact than those without the certification?

> Board-certified teachers indicate several reasons that lead them to seek the certification—more respect as teachers, higher income, and improved teaching practices.

The research:
What is the status of National Board certification across the country?
- In 2008 there were almost 64,000 Board-certified teachers, nearly triple the number in 2002.
- Twenty-five states had a 25 percent increase between 2006 and 2007 in the number achieving certification.
- Florida and North Carolina are the states with the highest numbers, in excess of 1,600 and 1,400 respectively.
- Ten percent of Board-certified teachers are in the fields of math or science.
- All states have access to funds to support teachers who seek NBPTS certification, and 27 of the 50 states provide financial incentives for teachers who complete the process. Almost all states have some type of incentive regarding certification or renewal of certification.

To measure the impact of Board-certified teachers on student learning, the NBPTS commissioned a number of independent research studies. Many of these, as cited on the Board Web site, reported favorable results.
- A University of Washington study reported that students with Board-certified teachers scored 7-15 percentage points higher on end-of-year tests than students of non-certified teachers. Effect was particularly noticeable with minority students.
- An Arizona State University study reported that the learning gains by which students of Board-certified teachers exceeded those of students with teachers who did not hold the same certification amounted to about one extra month in school.
- A researcher for the CNA Corporation reported testing gains for ninth and tenth graders in mathematics, with particular benefits to special needs students and African-American and Hispanic students.

However, other studies have found no significant difference in achievement between students of Board-certified teachers and teachers without that certification.
- A study by Sanders and colleagues at the SAS Institute, using a model that controlled for more variables, found no difference in achievement between students of the two teacher groups.

- A study by researchers at the University of North Carolina, Greensboro, found no differences in patterns of achievement between students of Board-certified vs. non-certified teachers. The researchers did find that Board-certified teachers exhibited better planning practices and selected reading passages for instruction that were at a higher cognitive level.

Practical implications:
- Some of the states that have limitations on financial incentives require that Board-certified teachers teach in schools with high needs in order to qualify for the extra pay. The value of such placement is supported by results from studies such as the University of Washington and CNA that have found Board-certified teachers produce higher scores in students of greater need.
- The Sanders study at the SAS Institute found variations were large within both groups of teachers—Board-certified and those without Board certification, so a child assigned to a Board-certified teacher was no more likely to get an effective teacher than if that child had been assigned to a teacher without that credential.
- Board-certified teachers indicate several reasons that lead them to seek the certification—more respect as teachers, higher income, and improved teaching practices. While those teachers may not initially aspire to leadership roles, the expectation has been established that these teachers will become leaders. However, appropriate training for the leadership roles thrust upon the newly Board-certified teachers is not always provided.

Questions to ask ourselves:
- Have we as a district collaborated with NBPTS certified teachers within the district to determine the most effective way in which the expertise of these teachers can be used?
- Have we as a district considered what kind of support can be provided for teachers seeking to achieve Board certification?
- If the state does not provide financial incentives, are district rewards for attaining certification feasible?

Resources:

McCloskey, Wendy, et. al. "Teacher Effectiveness, Student Achievement, & National Board Certified Teachers." 2005. 29 July 2008 <http://www.nbpts.org/UserFiles/File/Teacher_Effectiveness_Student_Achievement_and_National_Board_Certified_Teachers_D_-_McColskey.pdf>.

National Board for Professional Teaching Standards. "National Board Certification Statistics." 2007. 29 July 2008 <http://www.nbpts.org/about_us/2007_national_board_cert1/national_board_certifica/>.

Sanders, William, James Ashton, and Paul Wright. "Comparison of the Effects of NBPTS Certified Teachers with Other Teachers on the Rates of Student Academic Progress." Mar. 2006. 29 July 2008 <http://www.nbpts.org/UserFiles/File/SAS_final_NBPTS_report_D_-_Sanders.pdf>.

Wade, Carolyn, and Bill Ferriter. "Will You Help Me Lead?" *Educational Leadership* (Sept. 2007): 65-68.

Section IX: Health Issues

RESEARCH TIP #35
Obesity and Physical Education

The issue:
The National Association for Sport and Physical Education and the American Heart Association tell us that physically active, healthy kids learn better. The same groups report that school-age children and adolescents need at least 60 minutes of physical activity every day. However, the percentage of overweight children is growing at rapid rates, and evidence across the nation indicates that less time is being devoted to physical education as pressure increases to score well on high stakes assessments. What are the facts about overweight children and the extent of physical education in U.S. schools?

> A majority of the states (36 in all) have state requirements for physical education, but most do not set minimum instructional time allocations.

The research:
While the terms "obese" and "overweight" are applied to adults, "overweight" and "at risk of being overweight" are terms applied to children and teenagers. Both healthy and unhealthy weights are determined by body mass index (BMI), with gender, age, and height considered in determining categories. Young people with BMI in the 95th percentile or above are considered overweight, while those with a BMI between the 85th and 95th percentiles are considered at risk of being overweight. What are the statistics for American youth in these categories, and what are the inherent dangers?

- Sixteen percent of young people between six and 19—more than nine million—are overweight or at risk of being overweight. This rate has tripled since 1980.
- The percentage of overweight children and teens is considerably higher in the Hispanic and African-American communities.
- Overweight children are highly likely to be overweight or obese as adults. Studies indicate that approximately 80 percent of young people who were overweight between the ages of 10 and 15 were obese adults.
- Health risk factors that are more likely to occur in overweight children (as well as adults) include high blood pressure, high cholesterol, Type 2 diabetes, asthma, and sleep apnea.

Recent research indicates that many parents of overweight children do not see their children as having a weight problem. Fewer than one-half of parents with overweight children considered their children to be overweight. Adolescents involved in the same study were also unrealistic about their weight. Approximately one-third of overweight adolescents considered themselves in that category.

Increased physical activity, in addition to reduced caloric intake, is an important factor in preventing and treating weight problems. Schools and school districts have some influence over both factors, especially in the area of physical activity. What do the data tell us about physical education in U.S. schools?

- Forty-seven states have state standards for physical education, and 15 states require some type of student assessment in physical education.
- State standards do not translate into mandated programs. A majority of the states (36 in all) have state requirements for physical education, but most do not set minimum

instructional time allocations. Others have provisions that weaken expectations, such as allowing online completion of physical education requirements.
- Eleven states have minimum time requirements at the elementary level, ranging from less than 30 minutes a week (one state) to 150 minutes or more (two states). At the middle school level, seven states establish minimum requirements, as do 10 states at the high school level. Time requirements at those levels are higher than those for elementary school.

The National Center for Chronic Disease Prevention and Health Promotion, in its description of a coordinated school health program, includes physical education as one of the eight components of such a program. The Center specifically outlines a well-articulated K-12 curriculum that provides learning in a variety of physical activities taught by a qualified physical education teacher.

Practical implications:
- Include physical education at all levels as part of the K-12 educational program.
- Establish district-wide time allotments at the elementary level and require completion of some physical education courses at both the middle and high school levels.
- Incorporate physical activity throughout the day, including active recess time at the elementary level.

Questions to ask ourselves:
- As a school district, what minimum requirements for physical education time have we established—even if the state in which we reside does not have any?
- At the school level, how do we move beyond physical education requirements to provide our students with opportunities for moderate to vigorous exercise during each day?

Resources:
Center for Disease Control. "About BMI for Children and Teens. Undated. 2 July 2008 <http://www.cdc.gov/nccdphp/dnpa/bmi/childrens_BMI/about_childrens_BMI.htm>.
National Association for Sport and Physical Education. "Shape of the Nation Report." 2006. 2 July 2008 <http://www.americanheart.org/downloadable/heart/1154607764279ShapeOfTheNation.pdf>.
National Center for Chronic Disease Prevention and Health Promotion. "Coordinated School Health Program." 2007. 2 July 2008 <http://www.cdc.gov/HealthyYouth/CSHP/>.
Reuters Health. "Teens, Parents May Not See a Weight Problem." 2008. 2 July 2008 <http://www.reuters.com/article/healthNews/idUSKIM95354620080219>.

RESEARCH TIP #36
Schools and Nutrition

The issue:
Tip #35 addressed physical exercise as one way to combat obesity. The National Center for Chronic Disease Prevention and Health Promotion, in its description of a coordinated school health program, includes nutrition services as well as physical education in the eight components of such a program. In addition, appropriate nutrition is another weapon in the battle against obesity. What is the status of food services in American schools, and what are some of the challenges school districts face in providing healthy food for the students they serve?

> Canadian researchers found that students with increased fruit and vegetable consumption along with fewer calories from fat were more likely to receive a passing score on literacy tests.

The research:
Research studies indicate that, in addition to a healthy diet's impact on obesity, a healthy diet also influences school performance.
- Canadian researchers found that students with increased fruit and vegetable consumption along with fewer calories from fat were more likely to receive a passing score on literacy tests. Large differences were statistically significant.
- A five-year study of Minnesota teenagers found the students who regularly ate breakfast weighed less and were more physically active than their counterparts who skipped breakfast. An estimated 25 percent of American children regularly skip the morning meal.
- Researchers estimate that just two percent of our country's children eat a diet that is healthy according to United States Department of Agriculture (USDA) standards.

Federally funded school meals are subject to specific nutrition standards regarding breakfast and lunch. These standards are set by Congress and the USDA. In addition, schools are now required to submit "school improvement plans" for their cafeterias.
- The USDA standards were implemented more than 30 years ago. Problems in children's diets that nutrition science has identified since that time are not addressed in the standards.
- In the fall of 2007, 92 percent of schools receiving federal funds filed health and wellness policies that included specific goals for each school's food program.
- More than 80 percent of the nutritionists filing those reports believed the improvement plans were resulting in healthier food choices for their students.

In addition, states have varying guidelines about meals served outside the school cafeteria at meal time. The Center for Science in the Public Interest has evaluated those plans on several criteria, including food and beverage nutrition standards, and found the following:
- On an A-F grading scale, two states received an A- and 20 received an F. Sixteen states received a B, while the remaining states received a C or a D.
- Twelve states out of 50 have comprehensive policies addressing both food and beverage that apply to all grade levels all day long at all places on a school's campus.
- Only a small number of states have restrictions on whole or two-percent milk, sports drinks, sodium content in food, or portion sizes. Just over half the states limit additional sugar in snack foods.

Some good news in school cafeteria practices is also evident. Since 2000 the Center for Science in the Public Interest has noted the following changes:
- The percentage of states with restrictions against junk foods in school vending machines quadrupled over a six-year period, up to 32 percent of the states. Thirty percent of school districts have similar restrictions.
- The number of schools offering fruits and salad à la carte has increased to at least three-fourths of schools at all levels, with higher numbers at middle and high schools.
- Anecdotal evidence from cafeteria managers indicates that changes to more healthy foods do not necessarily reduce student consumption.

Practical implications:
- Develop a school nutrition policy that addresses not only the foods served in the cafeteria but also nutrition education and a parent-outreach component. A research study in the mid-Atlantic region found this intervention reduced the obesity incidence by 50 percent.
- Include a salad bar in the cafeteria in schools at all levels. A contributing factor to obesity is the fact that children do not consume enough fruits and vegetables, and adding a salad bar has been found to have a significant impact on higher consumption.
- More nutritious foods may cost more. All food costs have risen dramatically in recent years, with government funding not keeping pace with those increases. School districts must find ways to fund greater costs while meeting the need to feed an increasing number of students.

Questions to ask ourselves:
- Does our school or district have a school nutrition policy in place? If so, does it need to be updated? If a policy is not in place, who should be responsible for developing one?
- Are we making a concerted effort to ensure that all of our students begin the day with a healthy breakfast? What kind of school-based measures need to be in place?

Resources:
Blackwell Publishing Ltd. "Children with Healthier Diets Do Better in School, Study Suggests." *Science Daily*. 22 Mar. 2008. 15 Mar. 2009 <http://www.sciencedaily.com/releases/2008/03/080320105546.htm>.
Dunham, Will. "Magically Delicious: Breakfast Keeps Teens Lean." 3 Mar. 2008. 3 July 2008 <http://www.reuters.com/article/healthNews/idUSN2945373220080303?feedType=RSS&feedName=healthNews>.
Kopkowski, Cynthia. "The Dish on School Food." *NEA Today* (Feb. 2008): 32-33.
National Center for Chronic Disease Prevention and Health Promotion. "Coordinated School Health Program." 2007. 2 July 2008 <http://www.cdc.gov/HealthyYouth/CSHP/>.
Wootan, Margo. "State School Foods Report Card 2007." 2007. 2 July 2008 <http://www.cspinet.org/2007schoolreport.pdf>.

Section X: Language and Literacy

RESEARCH TIP #37
International Language at the Elementary Level

The issue:
Opportunities to begin the study of an international language at an early age grew rapidly in the United States during the decades of the eighties and nineties as districts added second-language study to the elementary curriculum. Two factors have contributed to a significant reduction in these programs since the turn of the century: funding constraints and the pressure of No Child Left Behind legislation.

> Students who learn a second language tend to be more creative and have enhanced ability to solve complex problems.

The research:
Answers related to funding depend upon political decisions, but a considerable body of research indicates that the presence of an organized program for studying a second language at the elementary level may contribute to student achievement in academic areas.

- There is a positive correlation between proficiency in a second language and both cognitive ability and academic achievement.
- Students who experience instruction in two languages at a young age reach higher levels of cognitive development at an earlier age than students instructed in just one language.
- Multiple studies have found a correlation between learning a second language at the elementary school and higher scores on standardized tests at the same level.
- Greatest impact appears to be in the area of verbal skills, but some studies have also documented a positive correlation between language study and performance in mathematics.
- Research results indicate that vocabulary in English is enhanced by the study of another language.
- Students who study another language develop more positive attitudes toward both the language and speakers of that language.
- Students who learn a second language tend to be more creative and have enhanced ability to solve complex problems.
- Studies that have analyzed student performance in an international language at the high school level indicate that students who studied a language at the elementary level had stronger performance in listening, speaking, and writing at the high school level than those students without a similar experience in earlier grades.

A well-designed elementary international language program enhances teaching and learning in elementary classrooms in a variety of ways:

- International language instruction at the elementary level supports the core curriculum by using themes congruent to those in mathematics, science, social studies, and language arts.
- Elementary-level instruction uses a variety of strategies that meet many different learning styles.
- The focus on culture supports the teaching of social studies, which is another area receiving less attention because of the No Child Left Behind focus on language arts and mathematics.

Practical implications:
The American Council of Teachers of Foreign Languages lists 12 characteristics of effective elementary international language programs. A partial list of those characteristics includes the following:
- equal access for all students, regardless of ethnicity, socioeconomic status, or achievement status;
- an extended sequence of learning that begins at the elementary level and extends through middle and high school years;
- articulation of learning goals and content from beginning levels through high school;
- instruction and materials that are developmentally appropriate and aligned with program outcomes; and
- teachers who are certified in their respective languages and who are aware of the developmental needs of children at various grade levels.

Whether teaching a second language to children who are native English speakers or teaching English to English language learners, there are misconceptions to avoid:
- Learning a second language is not always easier for a younger child than an older child or adult. Because vocabulary is more limited and sentence structure less complex for young children, it may appear they are advancing more rapidly. Research does support the advantage that younger children have in learning correct pronunciation.
- Acquisition of a new language does not necessarily increase with the amount of time devoted to learning the language (such as immersion programs). What is more important is the quality of instruction in the new language and the connections made between the new language and the native language.
- All children do not learn a second language in the same way. Culture as well as individual personality and learning styles play a significant role.

Questions to ask ourselves:
- What are the issues related to resources—financial and human—that we must resolve in order to institute or maintain an elementary international language program?
- How can we develop or improve an international language program that provides vertical articulation in the curriculum, developmentally appropriate activities and materials, and support of the core curriculum?

Resources:
American Council of Teachers of Foreign Languages. "Characteristics of Effective Elementary School Foreign Language Programs." Undated. 2 Aug. 2008 <http://www.yearoflanguages.org/i4a/pages/index.cfm?pageid=3655>.

American Council on the Teaching of Foreign Language. "What Does Research Show about the Benefits of Language Learning?" Undated. 1 Aug. 2008 <http://www.discoverlanguages.org/i4a/pages/index.cfm?pageid=4524>.

Curtain, Helena. "Foreign Language Learning: An Early Start, ERIC Digest." 1990. 2 Aug. 2008 <http://www.ericdigests.org/pre-9218/start.htm>.

McLaughlin, Barry. "Myths and Misconceptions about Second Language Learning." 1992. 2 Aug. 2008 <http://www.ncela.gwu.edu/pubs/ncrcdsll/epr5.htm>.

RESEARCH TIP #38
International Language at the Secondary Level

The issue:
Many policy makers focus on the need for greater enrollment and higher achievement in science and mathematics courses. Others cite the increasing need for proficiency in a second language in today's rapidly shrinking world. Many of the issues addressed in Research Tip #37, such as funding and impact of No Child Left Behind, affect language at the secondary level as well as the elementary level, but additional information is available to assist in planning for international language at the high school level.

> Integration of the culture of the language being learned has a positive impact on a student's ability to communicate in the language and to function in the culture.

The research:
According to a 2007 survey taken by the Scripps Howard News Service:
- Nearly two-thirds of Americans wish they had taken more international language while in high school, compared with just a third who wished they had taken more math and two-fifths who wish they had taken more science.
- The same survey found that male and female adults who responded to the survey were virtually even in the number of math and science courses they had completed, but almost twice as many women as men had completed four years of a international language.
- Participants in the survey indicated that usefulness of the language increased with the number of years spent in language study. Individuals who completed four years of study found the language to be very useful at a rate twice as great as those who had completed just one year of the language.

Data related to the languages being taken by students in U.S. high schools include the following:
- The most popular languages are Spanish, taken by approximately five million students; French, where enrollment is about one-fourth the number taking Spanish; then German, Latin, Italian, Japanese, and Russian in much smaller numbers.
- Languages considered most critical by U.S. government agencies are Chinese, Russian, and a number of languages spoken in mid-Eastern countries, such as Arabic and Farsi.

As of February 2008, 15 states had or were considering some type of graduation requirements for the study of an international language for all students.
- In many cases the proposals or legislation already enacted include the study of a language in a list of options leading to graduation.
- New Jersey education code requires the study of world languages at the elementary level.
- In some instances, state legislation that requires demonstration of proficiency in a language includes alternatives for local districts in the way programs are designed and the manner in which students demonstrate their mastery of a second language.

Much of the research cited in Tip #37 related to second language learning and academic achievement applied to learning at the secondary level as well. Additional research applicable to

both English language learners and native English speakers learning a second language provides the following information:
- At the secondary level a correlation has been found between the study of another language and higher levels of performance on both the ACT and the SAT.
- Students develop oral language proficiency more quickly when they have ample opportunity to interact with one another.
- Practice set in a meaningful context builds communication skills in an international language.
- Instruction in both writing and formal grammar needs to take into consideration both the skill level of students and the students' needs.
- Integration of the culture of the language being learned has a positive impact on a student's ability to communicate in the language and to function in the culture.

Practical implications:
Students who are more successful than others in learning a new language effectively choose and use learning strategies. A limited sample of the language learning strategies cited by Diaz include the following:
- Memory strategies: students create links through association, context, imagery, or physical activity; they engage in systematic, structured review over time.
- Cognitive strategies: students practice in a variety of formats, combine simple ideas and vocabulary into more complex sentences, break a new expression down into its parts, and compare new ideas in the second language with similar ideas in the student's first language.
- Compensation strategies: students ask for help, use their native language, simplify the message, and choose a topic for oral or written communication that fits their ability level.

Questions to ask ourselves:
- Do counselors and other staff members have appropriate information to use in advising students about the advantages of international language enrollment?
- Do we, as language teachers, have a consistent approach to teaching learning strategies to enable students to access and retain a language?
- In our language classrooms do we provide ample opportunity for students to interact and practice speaking and listening skills?

Resources:
Diaz, Miriam. "Learning Strategies in the Secondary Foreign Language Classroom: An Essential Curriculum Component for Beginning Students." 2004. 2 Aug. 2008 <www.wm.edu/education/599/04projects/Diaz.pdf>.

Hargrove, Thomas, and Guido Stempel. "Americans Wistful for Foreign Language in High School." 20 June 2007. 2 Aug. 2008 <http://newspolls.org/story.php?story_id=65>.

Kittock, Janice, and Ryan Wertz. "World Language Graduation Requirements." 2008. 1 Aug. 2008 <http://www.ncssfl.org/reports2/States%20with%20Foreign%20Language%20Requirements.doc>.

Manzo, Kathleen. "Students Taking Spanish, French: Leaders Pushing Chinese, Arabic." *Education Week* (29 Mar. 2006): 1+.

Met, Miriam. "Chapter 4. Foreign Language." *Handbook of Research on Improving Student Achievement, 2nd edition*, Gordon Cawelti, editor. Arlington, VA: Educational Research Service, 1999.

RESEARCH TIP #39
The Status of Writing

The issue:
"In most cases, writing ability could be your ticket in . . . or it could be your ticket out." This statement, from a corporate executive responding to a survey conducted by the National Commission on Writing, emphasizes the importance of writing in the business world as well as the academic world. This tip summarizes the status of writing in American schools, while the succeeding tip focuses on attributes of good writing programs.

> A survey of 120 major corporations indicated that writing is a "threshold skill" for both hiring and promotion of salaried workers.

The research:
The National Assessment of Educational Progress (NAEP) provides the best national description of the writing skills of American students in both public and private schools. The descriptor of proficient performance says students should be able to write a response that is organized, contains details to support the central idea, uses a variety of words and sentence structure, and has few mechanical errors.

The NAEP writing assessment was administered to a representative sample of students nationwide at grades four, eight, and 12 in 1998 and 2002 and in grades eight and 12 in 2007. Data from these administrations provide the following results:
- The percent of students demonstrating proficiency in writing was 28 percent at grade four in 2002. In 2007, 33 percent of eighth grade students and 24 percent of twelfth grade students participating in the assessment were at the proficient level.
- The average scale scores on the eighth grade writing assessment have increased three points at each administration, a statistically significant gain.
- Statistically significant growth has been evident for white, black, and Hispanic students, with a slight narrowing of the achievement gap.
- At grade 12 the scale score was higher in 2007 than in previous years by a statistically significant margin. The 2007 results indicate an upturn after 2002 scores decreased from 1998.
- At grade 12 significant gains were evident for white and black students. A small positive increase for Hispanic students was not statistically significant. There was no narrowing of the achievement gap between ethnic groups.

Survey data linked to student scores on the NAEP in both reading and writing, as summarized by Applebee, provide additional information:
- Almost 60 percent of teachers involved in administering the NAEP reported they spent less than 40 percent of their English language arts time on writing, while 11 percent spent 10 percent or less. Time declined between 2002 and 2005.
- Across different subgroups, higher achievement in writing was evident when teachers spend about half their instructional time helping students learn how to write.
- Frequent experiences in writing requiring analysis and interpretation are associated with higher writing scores for grade 12 students; however, just a third of seniors reported that this occurred frequently.

- Higher writing scores were associated with greater usage of computers for writing.

Information available from other sources provides additional information about the need for a focus on writing:
- A recent study showed that half of all freshmen entering the multiple state university campuses in California needed remedial help in English. Another survey indicated that almost all two-year public institutions of higher learning and two-thirds of four-year public institutions offered courses in remedial writing.
- A survey of 120 major corporations indicated that writing is a "threshold skill" for both hiring and promotion of salaried workers.

Practical implications:
- Writing is a major component of state academic standards.
- Assessments mandated by No Child Left Behind legislation always include reading; inclusion of writing varies from state to state.
- Increased time has been allocated to reading and mathematics in many districts, but attention to writing does not always follow.

Questions to ask ourselves:
- Do we have a consistent process for measuring student writing proficiency and growth across grade levels, both collectively and individually?
- If we analyzed the amount of time spent in writing in our language arts classes, what would it be?
- Do the writing experiences we provide for students increase in rigor across grade levels to include more analysis and interpretation?
- How extensively have we integrated the use of technology into our writing program?

Resources:
Applebee, Arthur, and Judith Langer. "The State of Writing Instruction in America's Schools: What Existing Data Tell Us." 2006. 8 June 2008 <http://www.albany.edu/aire/news/State%20of%20Writing%20Instruction.pdf>.

National Center for Education Statistics. "The Nation's Report Card: Writing." 2008. 30 Aug. 2008 <http://nces.ed.gov/nationsreportcard/writing/>.

The National Commission on Writing. "Writing: A Ticket to Work . . . Or a Ticket Out." The College Board. 2006. 8 June 2008 <http://www.writingcommission.org/prod_downloads/writingcom/writing-ticket-to-work.pdf>.

Parsad, Basmat, and Laurie Lewis. "Remedial Education at Degree-Granting Postsecondary Institutions in Fall 2000." *Education Statistics Quarterly* (Aug. 2004). 8 June 2008 <http://nces.ed.gov/programs/quarterly/vol_5/5_4/4_4.asp#2>.

Salahu-Din, Debra, Hilary Persky, and Jessica Miller. "The Nation's Report Card: Writing 2007." 2008. 8 June 2008 <http://nces.ed.gov/pubsearch/pubsinfo.asp?pubid=2008468>.

RESEARCH TIP #40
Effective Writing Instruction

The issue:
"The quality of instruction students receive is a major determinant of their writing achievement, and the quality of instruction varies dramatically." Thoughtful educators find no room for argument in this statement from "An Introduction to Writing" cited at the end of this tip. On the other hand, no teacher starts his or her work day with the intent of providing students with poor instruction in any content area, including writing. The question, then, is "What constitutes a high-quality writing program?"

> Development of writing skills is tied to reading; extended reading experiences result in stronger and more diverse writing.

The research:
Researchers have identified specific shortcomings of poor writers that include the following:
- Inadequate knowledge of text structure and organization.
- Less background about assigned writing topics than more proficient writers.
- Limited language skills such as vocabulary and sentence structure.
- Insensitivity to intended audience.
- Lack of planning or revising.
- Little faith in own competence as a writer.
- Little perseverance in the writing process.

A number of well-known models for writing exist. Key attributes of these models include skills such as these:
- An established routine for writing that is sustained, allowing students to become comfortable with the writing process.
- A shared and mutually understood language for setting expectations and giving feedback, including rubrics used by the teacher for feedback and for self-evaluation by the student writer.
- Specific instruction in three elements of writing: process strategies, such as prewriting, drafting, and editing; craft elements, such as character development; and mechanics of writing, including spelling, punctuation, and grammar.
- Consistency in expectations for writing and the type of instruction across grade levels and curricular areas.
- Differentiated instruction and support in the writing process for struggling students, with specific attention to identified shortcomings described in the previous list.

Practical implications:
Writers and teachers of writing have identified three different kinds of writing.
- Transactional writing, which may persuade, inform, or instruct; it is a means to an end.
- Expressive writing, which allows a writer to share thoughts and feelings.
- Poetic writing, in which language is used as an art form and the product is an end unto itself.

Several research findings relate directly to the different types of writing.
- Different forms of writing require different instruction and different processes.
- Development of writing skills is tied to reading; extended reading experiences result in stronger and more diverse writing.
- There needs to be a balance in the different types of reading and writing to which students are exposed.

In 2003 the National Council of Teachers of English (NCTE) initiated an extensive, nationwide campaign to assist schools and teachers within those schools in developing more proficient writers. One recommendation of the Council is that districts establish a comprehensive writing policy that defines writing expectations as well as processes that will help ensure the meeting of those expectations. Specific suggestions by NCTE include, but are not limited to, the following:
- Include in policy the expectation that all teachers—all grade levels and all content areas—share the responsibility for developing writing abilities appropriate for the age or course.
- Provide teachers with professional development in the teaching of writing. This training should extend across grade levels and content areas.
- Include in writing assignments a broad range of experiences with different purposes for writing.
- Incorporate technology both as a tool to support student writing and for students to present their learning in a variety of ways.

Questions to ask ourselves:
- What kind of policies or guidelines do we have as a district or school to direct the teaching and learning of writing?
- Do we provide adequate instruction in the writing process as well as time to apply that process?
- Are the types of writing tasks we present to students balanced, so students have the opportunity to experience and practice writing for a variety of purposes?
- Do our professional development opportunities and requirements extend to all teachers across grade levels and content areas?

Resources:
The Access Center. "Teaching Writing to Diverse Student Populations." Undated. 8 June 2008 <http://www.k8accesscenter.org/writing/documents/TroiaWritingDocument.pdf>.
National Council of Teachers of English. "Writing Now: A Policy Research Brief." 2008. 15 Mar. 2009 <http://www.ncte.org/library/NCTEFiles/Resources/Magazine/Chron0908Policy_Writing_Now.pdf>.
University of Kansas. "An Introduction to Writing." *Special Connections*. Undated. 8 June 2008 <http://www.specialconnections.ku.edu/cgi-bin/cgiwrap/specconn/main.php?cat=instruction&section=main&subsection=writing/main>.

RESEARCH TIP #41
Writing across the Curriculum

The issue:
The National Commission on Writing, a 20-member panel commissioned by the College Board, issued a report in early 2003 that lamented the state of writing in the United States. At the K-12 level, educators cite the demands to improve skills in reading and mathematics, which reduce time for writing. Writing to Learn and Writing across the Curriculum (WAC) have gained prominence as vehicles for improving students' writing as well as increasing content knowledge. What information does research provide about the extent of writing deficiencies and the viability of WAC as a partial solution?

> Writing in the content area—whether private journaling or product development—enhances learning and retention of the content, results in deeper understanding of the vocabulary and conventions of the discipline, and contributes to improved writing skills.

The research:
Research data from the National Commission on Writing and other sources indicate the following:
- As indicated in Tip #39, writing proficiency rates on the latest National Assessment of Educational Progress range between 24 percent and 33 percent. At the other end of the spectrum, more than 10 percent of eighth grade students and almost 20 percent of high school seniors did not possess even basic writing skills.
- College and university instructors report that about half of their students produce work that is free of conventional errors; these instructors also cite inability of students to analyze and synthesize information in their written work.
- K-12 educators cite emphasis on reading and mathematics and reliance on multiple choice tests as a barrier to teaching writing; however, the majority of states require writing samples in their testing programs.

Research studies over the last 35 years provide insight about WAC (including Writing to Learn) as a tool for addressing both writing skills and content knowledge:
- Writing to Learn and Writing across the Curriculum are most effective as strategies when they are a shared responsibility, i.e. not left to language arts teachers.
- Writing in the content area—whether private journaling or product development—enhances learning and retention of the content, results in deeper understanding of the vocabulary and conventions of the discipline, and contributes to improved writing skills.
- Students in Milwaukee schools that emphasized nonfiction writing showed significant gains in reading, mathematics, and science, even though time allocated to science had been reduced. Other studies (covering primary grades through college courses) cite gains in mathematics, reading, and science in schools or classes where additional time was devoted to writing.
- The need for reteaching and review is reduced when writing is incorporated into content areas, freeing up the time required for writing.

Researchers comparing differences in classroom instruction for schools with high levels of proficiency in writing versus schools with low proficiency found common characteristics in the

high proficiency schools. Some characteristics apply more specifically to English classrooms, while some are relevant to other content areas engaged in WAC.
- Teachers used varying strategies to help students learn; one strategy involved writing about a new concept in a variety of different ways.
- Teachers made specific connections between the content being studied and the writing assignment.
- Good writing assignments were based on specific and significant material.
- Good writing assignments provided specific suggestions in how to structure the assignment.
- Students were more engaged in the writing when they had some choices as to how the assignment should be completed.

Practical implications:
- Most studies cite correlation rather than causation when discussing the relation of WAC and increased content knowledge. Nevertheless, the evidence appears to support WAC as a viable, double-duty strategy for improving both writing and content knowledge.
- Extensive and ongoing staff development is needed for faculty members in all content areas regarding both the writing process and how to evaluate writing.
- The National Writing Commission recommends comprehensive policies about writing at the state level. Policies as well as explicit expectations about writing are also needed at the local level.

Questions to ask ourselves:
- As a school faculty, do we have clear expectations for Writing across the Curriculum as an instructional strategy?
- What staff development do we need to enhance our skills?
- What evaluation processes do we have in place to track the effectiveness of WAC?

Resources:
Danielson, Lana. "The Improvement of Student Writing: What Research Says." 2000. 15 Mar. 2009 <http://www.icsac.org/jsi/2000v1i1/improvement>.
National Center for Education Statistics. "The Nation's Report Card: Writing." 2008. 30 Aug. 2008 <http://nces.ed.gov/nationsreportcard/writing/>.
Reeves, Douglas. *Accountability in Action*. Denver, CO: Advanced Learning Press, 2000.
Shellard, Elizabeth, and Nancy Protheroe. *Writing across the Curriculum to Increase Student Learning in Middle and High School*. Arlington, VA: Educational Research Service, 2004.
The National Commission on Writing, "Writing and School Reform." The College Board. 2006. 24 Mar. 2008 <http://www.writingcommission.org/prod_downloads/writingcom/writing-school-reform-natl-comm-writing.pdf>.

RESEARCH TIP #42
Sustained Silent Reading

The issue:
Researchers in the field of reading consistently report that the more students read, the more competent they become as readers. In 1985 the Commission on Reading, in its report *Becoming a Nation of Readers*, recommended two hours a week of independent reading. Commission members recommended that time for this could be found by eliminating some of the time spent on skill sheets and workbooks. Proponents of Sustained Silent Reading (SSR) used this recommendation to support expansion of SSR programs. Yet in 2000 the National Reading Panel report stated there wasn't sufficient scientific evidence to support the use of SSR in schools. These disparate positions lead to the question, "What does the research tell us?"

> Studies have found that students who participate in planned free-reading programs (such as Sustained Silent Reading) do more independent, voluntary reading than students who do not participate in such programs.

The research:
Krashen describes three types of free voluntary reading: Sustained Silent Reading (SSR), in which both teachers and students participate in independent reading for a set amount of time each day or week; self-selected reading, in which teachers hold conferences with students to discuss what the students have read; and extensive reading, which has minimal accountability on the student's part. While some research has addressed the broader picture of free voluntary reading, SSR has received specific attention in many studies.

- The typical elementary school class spends less than 10 percent of its total reading instruction on independent silent reading.
- Surveys of elementary teachers indicate fewer than half of their schools incorporate SSR as standard operating procedure.
- Research has repeatedly shown a correlation between the amount of time spent reading and overall reading achievement, including vocabulary and fluency.
- Research on in-school free reading programs indicates such programs also have a positive impact on grammar and writing.
- An analysis of 54 studies that compared schools with planned free voluntary reading to schools without such a program found students in schools with the programs consistently did as well or better than students without such a program.
- Positive effects were found in 25 of the studies, with duration of the program having a direct impact on student achievement results.
- One study that found little difference in overall achievement found that statistically significant differences were apparent when students interacted with one another to discuss what they had read.
- Studies have found that students who participate in planned free-reading programs (such as Sustained Silent Reading) do more independent, voluntary reading than students who do not participate in such programs.
- One study that included a follow-up of adolescent boys found that the students who had participated in an extended free reading program were reading more six years later than students who had not participated in such a program.

- Studies that have analyzed how students actually use their time during Sustained Silent Reading (SSR) have found that 90 percent or more of the students were involved in reading. The involvement was highest when books from which students could choose were provided in the classroom, when teachers actively promoted some books, and when the teachers themselves were involved in reading during SSR.
- International studies comparing the reading skills of children in more than 30 countries found two consistent factors among those with the highest reading scores: they were students who were read to daily by their teachers and who read the most pages independently for pleasure.

Practical implications:

SSR programs that have contributed to improved reading skills in participating students have common attributes:
- The program is of sufficient duration to make an impact. Those programs that lasted six months or more had the greatest effect. Researchers indicate it may take four to five months to get students engaged in the process.
- A wide variety of materials is available, addressing both interest levels and readability. Students are allowed to choose what they want to read unless a selection is totally inappropriate.
- Teachers and other staff members serve as role models. All adults read during the SSR time. Teachers are enthusiastic about their reading and encourage reading for pleasure on the part of their students.
- The environment for SSR is conducive to quiet, uninterrupted reading.

Questions to ask ourselves:

- What steps do we need to take to implement an SSR program in our school? Are staff members supportive of such a program? Do we have the variety of reading materials we need to launch such a program? How would we evaluate the effectiveness of the program?
- If we already have an SSR program do we know if it is achieving the desired results? How can we determine the answer to that question?

Resources:

Anderson, Richard, Elfrieda Hiebert, Judith Scott, and Ian Wilkinson. *Becoming a Nation of Readers: The Report of the Commission on Reading*. Washington, DC: The National Institute of Education, 1985.

Binkley, Marilyn. "Becoming a Nation of Readers: What Principals Can Do." 1989. 8 July 2008 <http://eric.ed.gov/ERICDocs/data/ericdocs2sql/content_storage_01/0000019b/80/1e/35/ce.pdf>.

Krashen, Stephen. *The Power of Reading: Insights from the Research*. Portsmouth, NH: Heinemann, 2004.

Trelease, Jim. "Chapter 5: Sustained Silent Reading—Reading Aloud's Natural Partner." *The Read-Aloud Handbook*. 2006. 15 Mar. 2009 <http://www.trelease-on-reading.com/rah-ch5.html>.

RESEARCH TIP #43
Reading Aloud: Teachers and Parents

The issue:
"The single most important activity for building the knowledge required for eventual success in reading is reading aloud to children." This research-based conclusion from the 1985 report of the Commission on Reading (Anderson, p. 23) has been a catalyst for increased attention to a practice that was coming into its own as an instructional strategy a quarter of a century ago. What does more recent research tell us about the prevalence of the practice and its impact as a teaching and learning tool?

> Children who are read to regularly whether at home or school make large gains in both vocabulary and reading comprehension when compared to children who are not read to on a regular basis.

The research:
- The prevalence of reading aloud has increased dramatically over time. The proportion of elementary teachers who reported they read aloud to their students before the Commission on Reading's report was less than half. A study completed in 2000 indicated that 100 percent of elementary teachers reported they read aloud to their students on a regular basis (Kaplan, p. 2).
- At middle school, where the reported incidence of teachers reading aloud to students is much lower, students themselves report that listening to their teachers read aloud is a favorite literacy activity.

Jim Trelease, in *The Read-Aloud Handbook*, cites four specific benefits for reading aloud:
- Reading aloud conditions a child's brain to associate reading with pleasure. Identifying reading as an activity or experience that brings pleasure contributes to increased reading; increased reading, in turn, leads to more highly developed reading skills.
- Reading aloud creates background knowledge.
- Reading aloud builds vocabulary.
- Reading aloud provides a reading role model (Trelease, Chapter 1, page 2).

A summary of research from Krashen related to the benefits of reading aloud includes the following findings:
- The positive impact of reading aloud to children begins with experiences in the home and at the preschool level.
- Several studies indicate that children read more independently when they have been read to at home. In such cases, parents appear to have established routines for reading to their children starting at an early age.
- Classroom teachers may not be able to influence what happens at home or in preschool experiences, but they can use reading aloud in their classrooms to produce positive results.
- Children who are read to regularly whether at home or in school make large gains in both vocabulary and reading comprehension when compared to children who are not read to on a regular basis.

- Children's vocabulary knowledge grows as a result of hearing stories with unfamiliar words. Words need to be heard more than once, with discussion of the meaning of individual words.
- Studies indicate that children like being read to. Specific time set aside in the school day for reading aloud has been found to be a motivational factor for students to complete other tasks. Students are more likely to select books for independent reading that have already been read to them than ones with which they are not familiar.
- A study in a remedial reading class at the college level found that even college level students enjoyed and benefited from being read to by the teacher. Benefits were measured by the number of books checked out for independent reading and results on a final essay; comparisons were made between classes in which students were read to and those in which they were not.

Practical implications:
- Hearing a teacher read a story enhances children's comprehension. However, just listening is not sufficient; children need to participate in discussion to understand unfamiliar words and to make predictions and inferences about the story.
- A study of second grade students found that students benefited more from listening to a story being read when they only listened, rather than being asked to listen while following the story in print. Observations by researchers indicated that students were not as focused when given the written material to follow.

Questions to ask ourselves:
- What proactive measures have we taken to encourage and support parents of preschoolers in establishing read-aloud practices at home?
- Have we established consistent practices in our school for reading aloud to students, with appropriate time for interaction with students and attention to vocabulary development and comprehension?

Resources:
Anderson, Richard, Elfrieda Hiebert, Judith Scott, and Ian Wilkinson. *Becoming a Nation of Readers: The Report of the Commission on Reading*. Washington, DC: The National Institute of Education, 1985.

Binkley, Marilyn. "Becoming a Nation of Readers: What Principals Can Do." 1989. 8 July 2008 <http://eric.ed.gov/ERICDocs/data/ericdocs2sql/content_storage_01/0000019b/80/1e/35/ce.pdf>.

Kaplan, Julie, and Diane Tracey. "Teacher Read-Alouds at 2nd Grade, with and without Student Companion Texts: Unexpected Findings." 2007. 9 July 2008 <http://eric.ed.gov/ERICDocs/data/ericdocs2sql/content_storage_01/0000019b/80/3d/e0/8a.pdf>.

Krashen, Stephen. *The Power of Reading: Insights from the Research*. Portsmouth, NH: Heinemann, 2004.

Trelease, Jim. "Chapter 1: Why Read Aloud?" *The Read-Aloud Handbook*. 2006. 15 Mar. 2009 <http://www.trelease-on-reading.com/rah-ch1.html>.

RESEARCH TIP #44
Libraries and Learning

The issue:
Reading enjoyment has a strong relationship with student achievement. In a Canadian study, the presence of a school librarian was found to be the single greatest predictor of reading enjoyment for students at the elementary level. As a result of an Ohio survey of students across that state, Ross Todd states that "When effective school libraries are in place, students do learn. 13,000 students cannot be wrong" (Todd, p. 8.). How do school libraries and librarians bring about these kinds of affective and cognitive results in students?

> Visits to the library as class groups, with specific attention to information literacy skills, have a positive impact on writing scores at the middle and high school levels.

The research:
A study of more than 650 Illinois schools at all levels—elementary, middle, and high school—in all parts of the state and representing a variety of demographics provided the following results. These findings were consistent across student ethnicity, teacher-pupil ratio, and per pupil spending. Socioeconomic factors were evident in some findings, but not all of them.
- Illinois librarians reported that 30-35 hours are available each week for flexible scheduling at the middle and high school levels, while just 16 hours are available at the elementary level.
- Students at elementary schools with more flexible schedules scored 10 percent higher in reading and 11 percent higher in writing on state assessment tests. More positive results were also evident at the middle and high schools with more flexible schedules, but the differences were not as large as at the elementary level.
- Higher library staffing was also found to impact achievement. Better staffing was correlated with a positive difference at the elementary level of 13 percent in reading and 17 percent in writing. The difference in writing at the middle school was 18 percent in favor of students who attended schools with better-staffed libraries.
- The size and age of a school's print collection, including books and periodicals, was correlated with higher achievement scores regardless of class size or students' ethnicity.

An Ohio study of schools with effective library programs looked at specific ways in which those libraries met student needs. Information was collected from more than 13,000 student surveys.
- More than 99 percent of students surveyed indicated school libraries and the services available in those libraries had been helpful to them in some way.
- "Finding and locating information" was the area that students ranked highest when evaluating their school libraries. A close second was use of computers both at school and at home.

Quantitative findings in a 2007 study in Indiana support other research studies related to libraries and student performance. Students in schools with strong library programs (i.e., more adequate staffing and more plentiful and up-to-date collections) performed at a higher level on state assessments than their counterparts in schools with weaker programs. The study controlled for the influence of socioeconomic status and ethnicity.

Practical implications:
What are specific practices that make a difference in schools with good library programs?
- Higher levels of collaboration between librarians and teachers at the high school level are associated with higher student scores on the ACT, which is taken by all eleventh graders in Illinois schools.
- Specific types of collaboration between high school librarians and other staff members include identification of specific materials requested by teachers, joint planning between teachers and librarians, co-teaching, and time spent on school committees such as school improvement teams. As librarians' time devoted to these activities increased, a corresponding increase in ACT scores was noted in the Illinois study.
- Visits to the library as class groups, with specific attention to information literacy skills, have a positive impact on writing scores at the middle and high school levels. The impact is particularly strong at the middle school level.

The Indiana study analyzed values and perceptions of staff members regarding the role of media specialists. The following were found to be true in higher-performing schools as compared with lower-performing schools:
- Principals valued collaboration between librarians and classroom teachers.
- Principals scheduled regular meetings between themselves and their librarians and involved librarians on key school committees.
- Librarians believed both principals and teachers understood the role that librarians could play in designing curriculum and delivering instruction.
- Teachers believed teaching of information literacy was more effective when teachers and librarians collaborated in the instruction.

Questions to ask ourselves:
- As a building principal, what value do I place on the services of our school librarian? Have I utilized that individual's expertise in seeking information? Have I encouraged and provided mechanisms for collaboration between the librarian and classroom teachers?
- As a classroom teacher, how can I maximize the support the school librarian can provide for me and my students? What kind of collaboration and co-teaching will be most feasible as well as effective?
- As a librarian, how can I best share with my colleagues the kind of learning support that I can provide for them and the students in our building?

Resources:
Lance, Keith Curry, Marcia Rodney, Christine Hamilton-Pennell. "Powerful Libraries Make Powerful Learners: The Illinois Study." 2005. 26 Aug. 2008 <http://www.islma.org/pdf/ILStudy2.pdf>.
Lance, Keith Curry, Marcia Rodney, and Becky Russell. "How Students, Teachers, and Principals Benefit from Strong School Libraries: The Indiana Study—2007." 2007. 15 Mar. 2009 <http://www.ilfonline.org/AIME/indata.htm>.
The Ontario Library Association. "School Libraries and Student Achievement in Ontario." 2006. 26 Aug. 2008 <http://www.accessola.com/data/6/rec_docs/137_eqao_pfe_study_2006.pdf>.
Todd, Ross. "Student Learning through Ohio School Libraries." 2003. 26 Aug. 2008 <http://www.oelma.org/StudentLearning/documents/OELMAResearchStudy8page.pdf>.

Section XI: Social Studies

RESEARCH TIP #45
The Status of Social Studies

The issue:
"An unintended consequence of No Child Left Behind" is a phrase heard or seen with increasing frequency in relation to a variety of educational concerns, one of which is the teaching of social studies. This research tip focuses on test and survey results, while the one to follow (Research Tip #46) will deal with effective instruction in the area of social studies.

> Time allocated for the teaching of fine arts, international language, and social studies is decreasing, with impact greater in high-minority schools.

The research:
Tests in social studies—civics, economics, geography, and U.S. history—are included in the National Assessment of Educational Progress (NAEP). Tests are administered at grades 4, 8, and 12. There has been a single test administration in economics (2006), two administrations in geography (1994, 2001) and civics (1998, 2006), and three administrations in U.S. history (1994, 2001, 2006). The National Assessment Governing Board (NAGB) has established three levels of achievement: basic, proficient, and advanced. Proficient has been identified by the NAGB as the minimum level at which all students should perform. Performance results from the most recent administration of these tests include the following:
- The rates of proficient or above on the 2006 civics tests were as follows: grade 4, 24 percent; grade 8, 22 percent; grade 12, 27 percent.
- The percent of grade 4 students whose scores were at the basic level or above on the civics test increased from 69 percent in 1998 to 73 percent in 2006. Higher performance was evident in several student groups: male, female, white, black, and Hispanic. No significant gains were recorded at grades 8 and 12 for any of the three achievement levels.
- In geography, the 2001 rates for proficient or above were 21 percent at grade 4, 30 percent at grade 8, and 25 percent at grade 12.
- Scores in geography were higher at grades 4 and 8 in 2001 than they were in 1994; there was no significant change at grade 12.
- Statistically significant increases on the average score in U.S. history were recorded at all three grade levels in 2006. The improved performance was the result of a higher proportion of students scoring at the basic level.
- The proportion of students scoring at proficient or above on the history test in 2006 was 18 percent at grade 4, 17 percent at grade 8, and 13 percent at grade 12.
- On the 2006 test in economics given only at grade 12, 42 percent of the students taking the test earned scores that classified them as proficient or above.
- Achievement gaps were evident by ethnicity and socioeconomic status in all test administrations; the gap had narrowed in some instances between the earliest administration and the most recent one.

In addition to "unintended consequences," another oft-heard phrase is "what gets tested gets taught." A summary compiled by the Education Commission of the States reveals the following regarding inclusion of social studies in state assessment programs:
- Eighteen of the 50 states do not have assessments in social studies. Of the remaining

32, 20 percent are in the process of developing assessments or have state statutes that permit their development.
- Just under half the states—24 of the 50—include social studies in the state accountability system.

In a survey commissioned by the Council for Basic Education, von Zastrow surveyed almost 1,000 elementary and secondary principals in four states regarding student access to a liberal arts program.
- Time allocated for the teaching of fine arts, international language, and social studies is decreasing, with impact greater in high-minority schools.
- Teaching time for social studies, civics, and geography is decreasing in K-5 schools while time for reading, writing, math, and science is increasing.
- Teaching time and staff development for social studies is increasing at the secondary level.

Practical implications:
- Inclusion of social studies in state assessment and accountability systems, as recommended by von Zastrow's report, can come only through action at the state level.
- The time allocated to the instruction of social studies at the K-5 level is a district decision that needs to be carefully considered.
- A survey by 800 registered voters indicated that 66 percent of the respondents believed that curriculum in our nation's schools needs to go beyond the basics of reading, writing, and mathematics.

Questions to ask ourselves:
- Has time for instruction in social studies been included in time allocations at the K-5 level in our district? If not, where can time be found to address content in geography, history, and civics?
- What steps are we taking at all grades and in all courses to raise students' knowledge of social studies above a basic level?

Resources:
Education Commission of the States. "Citizenship Education Inclusion in Assessment and Accountability Systems." 2008. 24 Mar. 2008 <http://mb2.ecs.org/reports/Report.aspx?id=107>.
Hoff, David. "Bush, Others Want Law to Go Beyond Basics." *Education Week* (17 Oct. 2007): 18+.
National Center for Education Statistics. "The Nation's Report Card: Civics 2006." 2007. 25 Mar. 2008 <http://nces.ed.gov/nationsreportcard/civics/>.
National Center for Education Statistics. "The Nation's Report Card: Economics 2006." 2007. 25 Mar. 2008 <http://nces.ed.gov/nationsreportcard/economics/>.
National Center for Education Statistics. "The Nation's Report Card: Geography 2001." 2002. 25 Mar. 2008 <http://nces.ed.gov/nationsreportcard/geography/>.
National Center for Education Statistics. "The Nation's Report Card: U.S. History 2006." 2007. 25 Mar. 2008 <http://nces.ed.gov/nationsreportcard/ushistory/>.
von Zastrow, Claus. *Academic Atrophy: The Condition of the Liberal Arts in America's Public Schools.* 2004. 24 Mar. 2008 <http://www.music-for-all.org/documents/cbe_principal_Report.pdf>.

RESEARCH TIP #46
Effective Instruction in Social Studies

The issue:
Tip #45 focused on data related to the status of social studies in American schools, with the promise that this tip would deal with effective instruction in the area of social studies. In the words of Shaver (p. 145), "A substantial base of research on the teaching of social studies—many studies with rigorous designs—is not available ... [because of this] research cannot provide mandates for social studies instruction." With that caveat in mind, this tip focuses on promising practices in social studies that are based on some of the best research available.

> A systematic, sequential program for teaching map skills at early grades provides students with information and tools they need in further study of social studies; students' spatial relations are also enhanced.

The research:
Most of the practices below are found in the summaries of sound instructional practices provided by Shaver and Osborne. Many similarities appear in the two summaries, and many of the practices apply to instruction in areas outside of social studies. Most of the research cited by both authors is dated in the last two decades of the twentieth century.

- National social studies standards stress outcomes requiring analysis and interpretation. In classrooms that are promoting these thinking skills, teachers engage students in questions or problems that go further than knowledge and comprehension of basic facts.
- Teachers focus on in-depth study of fewer topics rather than broad coverage of many topics.
- Primary sources are used often, rather than relying solely on a textbook.
- Classroom strategies used by teachers to develop a positive climate include clear expectations for student behavior; a variety of strategies, including ones that actively involve students in lessons; and cooperative learning activities.
- Critical thinking skills are taught explicitly, in part by a teacher's modeling of metacognition.
- Concepts are developed through clear definitions accompanied by both exemplars and non-exemplars of the concept.
- Classroom questions posed to students are clear and at the appropriate level for students in the classroom. Questions based on knowledge and comprehension can be structured to lead to questions that call for interpretation and analysis.
- A systematic, sequential program for teaching map skills at early grades provides students with information and tools they need in further study of social studies; students' spatial relations are also enhanced.
- Vocabulary development in social studies is especially important in the middle grades. Studies have indicated that poor readers in upper elementary and middle school have the greatest difficulty with abstract and content-specific words.

Recommendations from the National Clearinghouse for English Language Acquisition include the following strategies related to teaching social studies to English language learners (ELLs) at the secondary level:

- Allow students adequate time to achieve understanding of key concepts. Most ELLs have not had multiple years of exposure to social studies content, and the content taught in

U.S. schools is not part of their culture. Vocabulary development is even more crucial for these students than for the student population as a whole.
- Link students' prior knowledge to new concepts. Development of students' oral histories can be used as a means to connect U.S. historical concepts to stories that arise from the oral histories.
- Use multiple delivery strategies that include visuals and artifacts that support individual learning styles. ELL students can often bring artifacts that reflect their own culture and that can help make sense of particular historical periods.
- Use cooperative learning strategies to increase interaction with peers and to extend the ways in which information is delivered to ELL students.

Practical implications:
- Provide direct vocabulary instruction. Strategies include introduction of new words in pre-reading activities as well as student construction of "foldables" that allow each student to use his or her own words to paraphrase the definition and to draw pictures that illustrate the new word.
- If time for social studies instruction has been reduced, especially at the pre-high school grades, find ways to integrate the learning of social studies with reading and mathematics. The Arizona Geographic Alliance is just one resource with multiple ideas.

Questions to ask ourselves:
- Are we using drill and practice of facts as a means to move students on to interpretation and analysis of social studies concepts, rather than using the learning of facts as an end in itself?
- Are vocabulary development activities a regular part of our instruction?
- How are we integrating the teaching of social studies with other content areas?

Resources:
Anstrom, Kris. "Preparing Secondary Education Teachers to Work with English Language Learners: Social Studies." 1999. 30 July 3008 <http://www.ncela.gwu.edu/pubs/resource/ells/social.htm>.

Arizona Geographic Alliance. "GeoLiteracy and ELL Adaptations." Undated. 30 July 2008 <http://alliance.la.asu.edu/geoliteracy/general.html>.

Association for Supervision and Curriculum Development. "Social Studies Jockeys for Position in a Narrowing Curriculum." *Education Update* (May 2006): 1-2, 6.

Osborne, Cliff. "BETTER Social Studies: Building Effective Teaching through Educational Research." Undated. 30 July 2008 <http://eric.ed.gov/ERICDocs/data/ericdocs2sql/content_storage_01/0000019b/80/13/b9/9f.pdf>.

Shaver, James. "Chapter 10. Social Studies." *Handbook of Research on Improving Student Achievement, 2nd edition*, Gordon Cawelti, editor. Arlington, VA: Educational Research Service, 1999.

RESEARCH TIP #47
Service Learning

The issue:
According to the 2008 report from the National Youth Leadership Council, approximately 4.7 million American students, grades K-12, participate in service learning. Investment in specific service-learning programs is in the millions of dollars, with an estimated return in value to communities served that far exceeds the initial cost. Multiple questions can be asked about service learning, but this tip addresses two: What is service learning? and What are the documented benefits of service-learning programs?

> Low income students who participate in service learning appear to do better academically than those who do not participate. As a result, service learning may narrow the achievement gap.

The research:
The answer to the first question, What is service learning?, depends on whom you ask. The terms "community service" and "service learning" are often used interchangeably, when in actuality the two are different. Many more schools provide students with the opportunity for community service than with actual enrollment in service-learning programs. The definition used by the National Commission on Service Learning states that service learning is "a teaching and learning approach that integrates community service with academic study to enrich learning, teach civic responsibility, and strengthen communities" (Fiske, p. 3).

With the current emphasis on accountability under No Child Left Behind, data related to academic achievement are important indicators for any program. Research results related to academic achievement as well as other areas of impact for service-learning programs include the following:

Impact on academic achievement:
- Several studies have found that students participating in service learning, when compared with non-participants, had higher scores in social studies, writing, and language arts.
- Participants in service learning demonstrate a higher degree of cognitive engagement and more motivation to learn.
- Higher grade point averages and improved attendance have been found to be associated with service learning.
- Low income students who participate in service learning appear to do better academically than those who do not participate. As a result, service learning may narrow the achievement gap.
- Service learning has been effective in increasing achievement among at-risk students.

Impact on civics and citizenship:
- Studies of California schools involved in the state-sponsored service-learning programs indicate that participating students achieve a high level of proficiency on selected academic standards related to civics and citizenship. No comparisons have been provided with non-participants or with overall performance on social studies standards.
- The area of civic involvement has been more difficult to evaluate because civic

involvement is often not an intentional goal of service learning. When it is a specific goal, it appears to have the desired results at the high school level.

Social and personal impact:
Over time, impact of service learning in this area has been the most frequently researched and documented. Service learning has a positive correlation with increased self-efficacy and self-confidence, respect of differences in others, ability to work collaboratively, and avoidance of destructive behaviors. More recently, studies have focused on the following:
- Career exploration: Students who participate in service learning have stronger skills in planning and preparing for post-secondary education and careers than students who did not participate in service learning.
- Ethics: In these studies ethics were defined as a development of a strong sense of right and wrong and willingness to stand up for what is right. Statistically significant differences have been found favoring students who participated in service learning compared with those who did not.
- Resilience: Students involved in service-learning classes have been found to be more apt to resist use of alcohol and tobacco, to be at lower risk for dropping out of school, and to be less involved in misconduct.

Practical implications:
- Impact on academic achievement is directly correlated with the quality of the program, specifically the clarity of academic goals and the support of the service-learning experience in meeting those goals.
- The 2008 report of the National Youth Leadership Council provides standards and indicators for service-learning programs. Specific standards addressed include, but are not limited to, the duration of the program, the alignment with and support of specific instructional objectives, and collaboration with community-based organizations.

Questions to ask ourselves:
- Have we established clear goals for the service opportunities in our school, whether those programs are simply community service or actual service-learning programs?
- If our program is a service-learning program, have we clearly defined the academic goals that the program supports? Are the service activities clearly aligned with the goals?
- What processes for evaluation of our program do we have in place?

Resources:
Fiske, Edward B. *Learning in Deed: A Report from the National Commission on Service Learning*. Undated. 15 Mar. 2009 <http://www.wkkf.org/pubs/PhilVol/Pub3679.pdf>.
National Youth Leadership Council. "Growing to Greatness 2007: The State of Service Learning." 2007. 1 July 2008 <http://www.nylc.org/inaction_init.cfm?oid=3698>.
National Youth Leadership Council. "Growing to Greatness 2008: The State of Service Learning." 2008. 1 July 2008 <http://www.nylc.org/objects/publications/8030548_Body.pdf>.
RMC Research Corporation. "Impacts of Service-Learning on Participating K-12 Students. (Expanded)" 2007. 1 July 2008 <http://www.servicelearning.org/instant_info/fact_sheets/k-12_facts/impacts/expanded.php>.

Section XII: Classroom Management, Discipline, and Safety Issues

RESEARCH TIP #48
Cyber Bullies

The issue:
Bullying behavior is not a new phenomenon, but until recent years it has been limited primarily to schools and other public places. But today, due to the widespread use of technology, bullying has invaded the privacy of the home. Cyber bullying provides anonymity and means that students can be harassed 24 hours a day, seven days a week.

> While face-to-face bullying is more prevalent among boys, cyber bullies are more predominantly female.

The research:
Some researchers differentiate between cyber bullying and online harassment. These individuals hold that online behavior constitutes bullying only when it is connected with offline bullying. However, the Pennsylvania Attorney General takes a different view and defines cyber bullying in this way: "Cyber bullying is sending or posting harmful or cruel text or images using the Internet or other digital communication devices, including cell phones and PDAs (personal digital assistants)."

Specific forms of cyber bullying may include the following:
- sending a threatening email;
- including insulting or threatening comments in an instant message;
- using someone else's screen name and pretending to be that person while sending a message or posting a note in a chatroom;
- creating a Web site with narrative or pictures belittling others;
- forwarding messages or pictures that were supposed to be private; and
- sending repeated text messages to a cyber target's cell phone.

A 2004 survey of middle school students by i-SAFE provided the following information:
- 58 percent of students surveyed had been the online recipients of mean or hurtful things.
- 53 percent of students in the survey admitted to having said mean or hurtful things to someone else while online.
- 42 percent of the students said they had been bullied while online; the distinction between mean or hurtful things and bullying was not clarified.

A more recent poll cited by the West Regional Equity Network provides additional data:
- More than 30 percent of all teenagers and almost 20 percent of children between six and 11 reported they have had hurtful things said about them online.
- 10 percent of the teens and four percent of younger children were threatened with physical harm.
- Just half of the children in the 6-11 age bracket and less than one-third of the older children told their parents. Almost 20 percent of the students told no one about the bullying incidents.
- Younger children were as likely to receive bullying messages at school as they were at home, while at-home messages were much more prevalent for teenagers—70 percent at home, compared with 30 percent at school.

Other studies indicate that while face-to-face bullying is more prevalent among boys, cyber bullies are more predominantly female.

Practical implications:
What state legislatures are doing:
- Maryland lawmakers recently approved a bill that requires both the state board of education and local boards of education to develop policies to fight bullying and harassment that occur physically, verbally, or electronically.
- Missouri legislatures have revised the state's harassment laws to include electronic communications. Harassment on the Internet is now a felony offense in the state; the new legislation resulted from the suicide of a teenager who was insulted and mocked on a social networking site.

What can schools do?
- Update school board policy to address harassment via technology.
- Include a section on cyber bullying and district policy in the student handbook.
- Establish serious consequences for students who do not abide by the policy.
- Develop and implement a classroom-based anti-bullying program that includes cyber bullying.
- Block district-wide access to any personal email accounts or blog sites that cannot be monitored.

i-SAFE offers suggestions to students who are victims of cyber bullying:
- Tell a responsible adult, and keep telling until action is taken.
- If the bullying is school related, tell a school teacher or administrator.
- Don't respond to messages from cyber bullies.
- Don't erase messages; they can be used for evidence if action is taken.
- Call the police if a cyber bully threatens harm.

Questions to ask ourselves:
- Does our district have a bullying policy that includes cyber bullying?
- Have we taken necessary actions to reduce the opportunity for cyber bullying at school?
- Is cyber bullying addressed in our overall program to reduce or eliminate bullying behavior?

Resources:
i-SAFE America Inc. "Beware of the Cyber Bully." Undated. 25 July 2008 <http://www.isafe.org/imgs/pdf/education/CyberBullying.pdf>.
Pennsylvania Office of Attorney General. "Cyber Bullying." Undated. 25 July 2008 <http://www.attorneygeneral.gov/kidsparents.aspx?id=1567>.
West Regional Equity Network. "About Cyber-Bullying." 2008. 5 Mar. 2009 <http://uacoe.arizona.edu/wren/bully_cyber_about.html>.

RESEARCH TIP #49
Proactive Classroom Management

The issue:
A strong research base supports the statement that receiving high-quality instruction by an effective teacher is the most important school factor in a student's achievement. More than 30 years of research indicate that classroom management is a critical component, perhaps the most important component, of teacher effectiveness. Management of student behavior and instructional management are two sides of the classroom management coin. This research tip focuses on instructional management that encourages positive student behaviors and minimizes disruptive behavior; the next tip will deal more specifically with managing student behavior.

> Marzano's research indicated that the students of teachers trained in the use of classroom management techniques were more highly engaged and less disruptive than students in classrooms whose teachers had not had similar training.

The research:
Jacob Kounin conducted what may have been the first major study of effective classroom management in 1970. In that study he identified four major components of classroom management by effective teachers: "with-it-ness," pacing of lessons, establishment of student expectations, and quality of seatwork.

"With-it-ness" is a teacher's awareness of what is happening in the classroom at all times. While no specific action is attached to "with-it-ness," this awareness is a powerful tool in classroom management. Teachers who possess this attribute keep track of what is going on in the classroom, no matter what they are doing at the time, and students know the teacher is keeping track of their behavior. This allows teachers to intervene in potential disruptive behavior before that behavior escalates.

Initial support for strong classroom management on the part of teachers begins with attitudes and practices throughout the school.
- High expectations are established and communicated for both student performance and student behavior. All staff members are committed to these expectations.
- The school climate is positive and conveys a genuine interest in students and their welfare.
- The principal is highly visible in hallways and classrooms, talking with both teachers and students.
- Principals hold teachers accountable for classroom management, including student discipline, but provide support as needed.

Specific instructional strategies that contribute to good classroom management include the following:
- Classroom space is organized in such a way that students have a clear line of sight to instruction and the teacher has that same line of sight to all students, allowing for ease of monitoring. The classroom arrangement also allows for easy access by the teacher to any student in the room.

- Management strategies, including use of materials and student movement, are planned in advance and support the learning that is to occur.
- Students are actively engaged in learning from the beginning until the end of the day or the class period.
- Students are informed of the purpose of a lesson and where it is headed.
- Activities are matched to students' interests and abilities. This may call for differentiation in a heterogeneous classroom; all students may not benefit from the same activity.
- Lessons move at a pace that keeps students' interest and attention; teachers need to constantly monitor students' attention levels (i.e., practice "with-it-ness") and modify the pace as needed.

Marzano raised the question, "Are good classroom managers born or made?" He answered his own question by citing research indicating that teachers could learn strategies for classroom management in a relatively brief period of time. His research also indicated that the students of teachers trained in the use of classroom management techniques were more highly engaged and less disruptive than students in classrooms whose teachers had not had similar training.

Practical implications:
- Plan classroom arrangement with an eye to effective instruction; look for ways to modify the arrangement if a particular activity calls for a different setup.
- Begin class immediately, with the objective of the learning activity clearly communicated and understood by students.
- Be prepared with necessary teacher and student materials ready for use.
- Keep transition time to a minimum. This applies to teachers at all levels—to elementary teachers as they change from subject to subject, to middle and high school teachers as they change activities within a teaching period.
- Keep any lessons moving at a pace that keeps students engaged.
- Move among students to monitor their engagement and progress in the learning activity.

Questions to ask ourselves:
- How do I introduce a lesson to my students? Do I give them a clear picture of the purpose of the lesson and where it is headed?
- Does the pacing of my lessons keep students actively engaged? How can I modify lessons to maintain momentum and student interest?
- Does the arrangement of my classroom maximize students' ability to be actively engaged in the lesson as well as my ability to move about the classroom to monitor and assist?

Resources:
Cotton, Kathleen. "Schoolwide and Classroom Discipline." School Improvement Research Series, Close-Up #9. 2001. 26 July 2008 <http://www.nwrel.org/scped/sirs/5/cu9.html>.

Kounin, Jacob. *Discipline and Group Management in the Classroom*. New York: Holt, Rinehart, and Winston, 1970.

Marzano, Robert. *Classroom Management That Works*. Alexandria, VA: Association for Supervision and Curriculum Development, 2003.

Shellard, Elisabeth, Nancy Protheroe, and Jennifer Turner. *Effective Classroom Management to Support Student Learning*. Arlington, VA: Educational Research Services, 2005.

RESEARCH TIP #50
Dealing with Disruptive Behavior

The issue:
As noted in the previous tip, effective classroom management is a combination of sound instructional strategies and management of student behavior in a variety of ways. Tip #49 dealt with a proactive approach for management of instruction; this tip focuses on selected research findings related to discipline in the classroom.

> Students prefer teachers who deal directly with the situation but are not harsh or inflexible in the consequences.

The research:
How big an issue is discipline?
- A survey conducted by the U.S. Department of Education revealed that fewer than 20 percent of first-year teachers considered themselves well prepared to deal with classroom management and discipline.
- Thirty percent of teachers responding to a Public Agenda survey agreed that many teachers are not effective classroom managers.
- Results from the Gallup Poll consistently rate discipline as a major concern of respondents.

In *The Educator's Guide to Preventing and Solving Discipline Problems,* the Boyntons cite the 80-15-5 principle of classroom behavior: 80 percent of the students are consistently well behaved and follow the rules, 15 percent occasionally cause problems, and 5 percent are chronic problems. Based on the work of other researchers, the Boyntons outline four crucial discipline components and rank their relative importance (Boynton, p. 4):
- Positive student-teacher relationships: 40 percent
- Monitoring skills: 25 percent
- Clear parameters of acceptable behaviors: 25 percent
- Consequences: 10 percent

The establishment of positive student-teacher relationships begins with communication of high expectations and the equitable treatment of all students.

In analysis of numerous research studies, Kathleen Cotton has identified specific teacher actions that lead to desired student behavior in the classroom:
- Specific classroom rules and procedures have been established and posted in the classroom. At the early grades, those rules and procedures have been modeled and taught.
- Consequences for inappropriate behavior have been explained.
- Rules are enforced promptly, fairly, and with consistency.

Robert Marzano suggests teachers should use discipline actions and strategies that are based on assertiveness, not aggressiveness. High school principals have identified characteristics of teachers who deal well with disruptive behaviors. A review of those strategies indicates they are consistent

with Marzano's suggested pattern of assertiveness rather than aggressiveness. According to principals, teachers who are effective in their classroom discipline typically do the following:
- Establish behavioral expectations and enforce those expectations consistently and fairly.
- Deal with problems on their own, rather than sending students to someone else to handle the problem.
- Use movement in the classroom, with proximity to specific students as needed.
- Select the battles they choose to fight. Some issues are definitely more important than others.
- Respond quickly to defuse potential disruptions (awareness of potential disruption is based on "with-it-ness," as described in Tip #49).
- Have a plan of action (thought out in advance) for dealing with disruption when it does occur.
- Avoid power struggles with students.
- Analyze and change their own behavior if necessary.

What do students say about discipline?
- Students participating in a panel presentation at an ASCD conference indicated that one of the top qualities they desired in their respective schools was "positive discipline."
- Students prefer teachers who deal directly with the situation but are not harsh or inflexible in the consequences.

Practical implications:
- Demonstrate to students in a genuine way that you care about each one of them and expect each one to succeed.
- Develop appropriate classroom rules and procedures and implement them consistently.
- State rules in a positive way, describing the behavior you want to see rather than what students should not do.
- Temper disciplinary procedures with appropriate concern for students and their needs.

Questions to ask ourselves:
- Have I established and explained clear behavioral expectations for my classroom?
- Do I implement rules and procedures consistently and fairly?
- What changes in my own behavior might work toward minimizing confrontations and disruptions?

Resources:
Association for Supervision and Curriculum Development. "Listening to the Whole Child." *Education Update* (Jan. 2006): 1.

Boynton, Mark, and Christine Boynton. *The Educator's Guide to Preventing and Solving Discipline Problems*. Alexandria, VA: Association for Supervision and Curriculum Development, 2005.

Cotton, Kathleen. "Schoolwide and Classroom Discipline." School Improvement Research Series, Close-Up #9. 2001. 26 July 2008 <http://www.nwrel.org/scped/sirs/5/cu9.html>.

Marzano, R. *Classroom Management That Works*. Alexandria, VA: Association for Supervision and Curriculum Development, 2003.

Shellard, Elisabeth, Nancy Protheroe, and Jennifer Turner. *Effective Classroom Management to Support Student Learning*. Arlington, VA: Educational Research Services, 2005.

Resources

Books and Periodicals

Anderson, Richard, Elfrieda Hiebert, Judith Scott, and Ian Wilkinson. *Becoming a Nation of Readers: The Report of the Commission on Reading.* Washington, DC: The National Institute of Education, 1985.

Archer, Jeff. "Tackling an Impossible Job." *Education Week* supplement (15 Sept. 2004): S3+.

Archer, Jeff. "Theory of Action" and "Guiding Hand." *Education Week* supplement (14 Sept. 2004): S3+.

Association for Supervision and Curriculum Development. "Listening to the Whole Child." *Education Update* (Jan. 2006): 1.

Association for Supervision and Curriculum Development. "Social Studies Jockeys for Position in a Narrowing Curriculum." *Education Update* (May 2006): 1-2, 6.

Black, Susan. "What Did You Learn Last Summer?" *American School Board Journal* (Feb. 2005); 38-40.

Boynton, Mark, and Christine Boynton. *The Educator's Guide to Preventing and Solving Discipline Problems.* Alexandria, VA: Association for Supervision and Curriculum Development, 2005.

Caine, Renate, and Geoffrey Caine. *Teaching and the Human Brain.* Alexandria, VA: Association for Supervision and Curriculum Development, 1994.

Cech, Scott. "AP Trends: Tests Soar, Scores Slip." *Education Week* (20 Feb. 2008): 1+.

Cech, Scott. "College Board Intends to Drop AP Programs in Four Subjects." *Education Week* (9 Apr. 2008): 13.

Clarke, Suzanne. *ERS Focus on Educating Boys.* Arlington, VA: Educational Research Service, 2007.

Clarke, Suzanne. *Single-Sex Schools and Classrooms.* The Informed Educator Series. Arlington, VA: Educational Research Service, 2007.

Danielson, Charlotte. "Strengthening the School's Backbone." *Journal for Staff Development* (Spring 2005): 34-37.

David, Jane. "What Research Says about . . . /Grade Retention." *Educational Leadership* (Mar. 2008): 83-84.

Downey, Carolyn. *Participant's Manual. Conducting Walkthroughs to Maximize Student Achievement: Cutting Edge Practice Series.* Johnson, IA: Curriculum Management Services, Inc., 2001.

Dozier, Terry. "Turning Good Teachers into Great Leaders." *Educational Leadership* (Sept. 2007): 14-19.

Edwards, Virginia (Ed.). "Technology Counts 2002. E-Defining Education." *Education Week* (May 9, 2002).

Edwards, Virginia (Ed.). "Technology Counts 2006. The Information Edge: Using Data to Accelerate Achievement." *Education Week* (May 4, 2006).

Edwards, Virginia (Ed.). "Technology Counts 2007: A Digital Decade." *Education Week* (Mar. 29, 2007).

Ferrara, Peter, and Margaret Ferrara. "Single-Gender Classrooms: Lessons from a New York Middle School." *ERS Spectrum* (Summer 2004): 26-32.

Franklin, John. "Achieving with Autism." *Education Update*, Association for Supervision and Curriculum Development (July 2007): 1+.

Gabriel, John. *How to Thrive as a Teacher Leader.* Arlington, VA: Association for Supervision and Curriculum Development, 2005.

Hoff, David. "Bush, Others Want Law to Go Beyond Basics." *Education Week* (17 Oct. 2007): 18+.

Hollingsworth, John. Data Works Professional Development Conference for Principals. Los Angeles Unified School District, Sept. 2002.

Honawar, Vaishali. "Reports Renew Debate over Alternative Preparation." *Education Week* (19 Dec. 2007): 11.

Jacobson, Linda. "Support, Data Seen Key to Pre-K Teacher Effectiveness." *Education Week* (10 Oct. 2007): 11.

Jensen, Eric. *Enriching the Brain: How to Maximize Every Learner's Potential.* San Francisco, CA: Jossey-Bass, 2006.

Jensen, Eric. *Teaching with the Brain in Mind.* Alexandria, VA: Association for Supervision and Curriculum Development, 2005.

Johnson, Susan, and Morgaen Donaldson. "Overcoming the Obstacles to Leadership." *Educational Leadership* (Sept. 2007): 8-13.

Keller, Bess. "'Book Study' Helps Teachers Hone Skills." *Education Week* (21 May 2008): 1+.

Kopkowski, Cynthia. "The Dish on School Food." *NEA Today* (Feb. 2008): 32-33.

Kounin, Jacob. *Discipline and Group Management in the Classroom.* New York: Holt, Rinehart, and Winston, 1970.

Krashen, Stephen D. *The Power of Reading: Insights from the Research.* Portsmouth, NH: Heinemann, 2004.

MacIver, Martha, and Elizabeth Farley-Ripple. *Bringing the District Back In: The Role of the Central Office in Instruction and Achievement.* Alexandria, VA: Educational Research Service, 2008.

Manzo, Kathleen. "Students Taking Spanish, French: Leaders Pushing Chinese, Arabic." *Education Week* (29 Mar. 2006): 1+.

Marzano, Robert *Classroom Management That Works.* Alexandria, VA: Association for Supervision and Curriculum Development, 2003.

Marzano, Robert, Timothy Waters, and Brian McNulty. *School Leadership that Works: From Research to Results.* Arlington, VA: Association for Supervision and Curriculum Development, 2005.

Met, Miriam. "Chapter 4. Foreign Language." *Handbook of Research on Improving Student Achievement,* 2nd edition, Gordon Cawelti, editor. Arlington, VA: Educational Research Service, 1999.

Molineaux, Rebecca. *ERS Focus on Supporting English Language Learners in Mainstream Classrooms.* Arlington, VA: Educational Research Service, 2007.

Nichols, Beverly. *Improving Student Achievement: 50 Research-Based Strategies.* Columbus, OH: Linworth Publishing, Inc., 2008.

Owings, William, and Leslie Kaplan. "Standards, Retention, and Social Promotion." *NASSP Bulletin* (Dec. 2001): 57-66.

Porch, Stephanie, and Nancy Protheroe. *School Board-Superintendent Relations in Support of High Student Achievement*. The Informed Educator Series. Alexandria, VA: Educational Research Services, 2006.

Protheroe, Nancy. *School Boards Focused on Student Learning*. The Informed Educator Series. Alexandria, VA: Educational Research Services, 2003.

Raywid, Mary Anne. "Synthesis of Research/Small Schools: A Reform That Works." *Educational Leadership* (Dec. 1997/Jan. 1998): 34-39.

Reeves, Douglas. *Accountability in Action*. Denver, CO: Advanced Learning Press, 2000.

Rodriquez, Carmen, and Bernard Arenz. "The Effects of Looping on Perceived Values and Academic Achievement." *ERS Spectrum* (Summer 2007): 43-55.

Samuels, Christina. "'Response to Intervention' Sparks Interest, Questions." *Education Week* (23 Jan. 2008): 1+.

Sax, Leonard "The Promise and Peril of Single-Sex Public Education." *Education Week* (2 Mar. 2005): 48+.

Schweinhart, Lawrence. "Creating the Best Prekindergartens: Five Ingredients for Long-Term Effects and Returns on Investment." *Education Week* (19 Mar. 2008): 27+.

Shaver, James. "Chapter 10. Social Studies." *Handbook of Research on Improving Student Achievement, 2nd edition*, Gordon Cawelti, editor. Arlington, VA: Educational Research Service, 1999.

Shellard, Elizabeth, and Nancy Protheroe. *After-School Programs: A Strategy for Raising Student Achievement*. The Informed Educator Series. Alexandria, VA: Educational Research Service, 2006.

Shellard, Elisabeth, Nancy Protheroe, and Jennifer Turner. *Effective Classroom Management to Support Student Learning*. Arlington, VA: Educational Research Services, 2005.

Shellard, Elizabeth, and Nancy Protheroe. *Writing across the Curriculum to Increase Student Learning in Middle and High School*. Arlington, VA: Educational Research Service, 2004.

Sprenger, Marilee. *How to Teach So Students Remember*. Alexandria, VA: Association for Supervision and Curriculum Development, 2005.

Sprenger, Marilee. *Learning & Memory: The Brain in Action*. Alexandra. VA: Association for Supervision and Curriculum Development, 1999.

Sylwester, Robert. *A Celebration of Neurons*. Alexandria, VA: Association for Supervision and Curriculum Development, 1995.

Tomlinson, Carol Ann. *The Differentiated Classroom: Responding to the Needs of All Learners*. Alexandria, VA: Association for Supervision and Curriculum Development, 1999.

Viadero, Debra. "Evidence for Moving to K-8 Model Not Airtight." *Education Week:* (16 Jan. 2008): 1+.

Wade, Carolyn, and Bill Ferriter. "Will You Help Me Lead?" *Educational Leadership* (Sept. 2007): 65-68.

Resources—Electronic

The Access Center. "Teaching Writing to Diverse Student Populations." Undated. 8 June 2008 <http://www.k8accesscenter.org/writing/documents/TroiaWritingDocument.pdf>.

Alexander, Karl, Doris Entwisle, and Linda Olson. "Lasting Consequences of the Summer Learning Gap." 2007. 20 Apr. 2008 <http://www.asanet.org/galleries/default-file/April07ASRFeature.pdf>.

American Association of School Administrators. "After-School Programs: Bureaucratic Barriers and Strategies for Success." *School Governance and Leadership* (Fall 2005). 31 July 2008 <http://aasa.org/files/PDFs/Publications/SchGovLdrshp/SGLAfterschool.pdf>.

American Council of Teachers of Foreign Languages. "Characteristics of Effective Elementary School Foreign Language Programs." Undated. 2 Aug. 2008 <http://www.yearoflanguages.org/i4a/pages/index.cfm?pageid=3655>.

American Council on the Teaching of Foreign Language. "What Does Research Show about the Benefits of Language Learning?" Undated. 1 Aug. 2008 <http://www.discoverlanguages.org/i4a/pages/index.cfm?pageid=4524>.

Anstrom, Kris. "Preparing Secondary Education Teachers to Work with English Language Learners: Social Studies." 1999. 30 July 3008 <http://www.ncela.gwu.edu/pubs/resource/ells/social.htm>.

Applebee, Arthur, and Judith Langer. "The State of Writing Instruction in America's Schools: What Existing Data Tell Us." 2006. 8 June 2008 <http://www.albany.edu/aire/news/State%20of%20Writing%20Instruction.pdf>.

Arizona Geographic Alliance. "GeoLiteracy and ELL Adaptations." Undated. 30 July 2008 <http://alliance.la.asu.edu/geoliteracy/general.html>.

Autism Research Institute. "Developing Academic Accommodations Promoting Successful Inclusion." 2007. 18 Aug. 2008 <http://www.autism.com/individuals/9domains.htm>.

Barnett, W. Steven, et al. "Effects of Five State Prekindergarten Programs on Early Learning." 2007. 18 Aug. 2008 <http://nieer.org/docs/?DocID=129>.

Barnett, W. Steven, et al. *The State of Preschool 2007*. 2007. 18 Aug. 2008 <http://nieer.org/yearbook/>.

Bassett, Patrick. "Faculty Meeting Blues." 1996. 22 Apr. 2008 <http://www.isacs.org/resources/monographs/library.asp?id=241&category=11&action=show>.

Binkley, Marilyn. "Becoming a Nation of Readers: What Principals Can Do." 1989. 8 July 2008 <http://eric.ed.gov/ERICDocs/data/ericdocs2sql/content_storage_01/0000019b/80/1e/35/ce.pdf>.

Blackwell Publishing Ltd. "Children with Healthier Diets Do Better in School, Study Suggests." *Science Daily*. 22 Mar. 2008. 3 July 2008 <http://www.sciencedaily.com/releases/2008/02/080320105546.htm>.

Bodilly, Susan, and Megan Beckett. "Making Out-of-School Time Matter: Evidence for an Action Agenda." 2005. 31 July 2008 <http://www.rand.org/pubs/research_briefs/2005/RAND_RB9108.pdf>.

Bogart, Vada, "The Effects of Looping on the Academic Achievement of Elementary School Students." 2002. 18 Aug. 2008 <http://etd-submit.etsu.edu/etd/theses/available/etd-0820102-105005/unrestricted/BogartV082302a.pdf>.

Boss, Suzie, and Jennifer Railsback. "Summer School Programs: A Look at the Research, Implications for Practice, and Program Sampler." Sept. 2002. 20 Aug. 2008 <http://www.nwrel.org/request/2002sept/summerschool.pdf>.

Bottge, Brian, and John Gugerty. "Block Scheduling: Some Benefits but No Magic Fix." 2004. 12 Aug. 2008 <http://www.wcer.wisc.edu/news/coverStories/block_scheduling.php>.

Bright Solutions for Dyslexia, LLC. "Teaching Methods That Work." 1998. 23 Aug. 2008 <http://www.dys-add.com/teach.html>.

Bright Solutions for Dyslexia, LLC. "What Is Dyslexia?" 1998. 23 Aug. 2008 <http://www.dys-add.com/define.html>.

Brock, Stephen. "Special Needs: Helping the Student with ADHD in the Classroom." 2002. 21 Aug. 2008 <http://www.nasponline.org/resources/handouts/special%20needs%20template.pdf>.

Bromley, Anne. "Block Scheduling: Not Helping High School Students Perform Better in College Science." *Inside UVA Online* (Spring 2006). 12 Aug. 2008 <http://www.virginia.edu/insideuva/2006/08/block_scheduling.html>.

Caine, Renate, and Geoffrey Caine. "Overview of the Systems Principles of Natural Learning." Undated. 28 Aug. 2008 <http://cainelearning.com/files/Summary.pdf>.

California Department of Education. "Adolescent Development and Instruction, Assessment, and Intervention." Undated. 27 Aug. 2008 <http://pubs.cde.ca.gov/tcsii/ch2/adlescntdevchpt2.aspx>.

Center for Applied Research and Educational Improvement. "Research & Resources—Student Achievement." 2006. 12 Aug. 2008 <http://cehd.umn.edu/CAREI/Blockscheduling/Resources/StudentAcheivement.html>.

Center for Disease Control. "About BMI for Children and Teens. Undated. 2 July 2008 <http://www.cdc.gov/nccdphp/dnpa/bmi/childrens_BMI/about_childrens_BMI.htm>.

Center for Educational Networking. "NASDSE Explains Response to Intervention." *Focus on Results*. 2006. 24 Mar. 2008 <http://www.cenmi.org/focus/policy/august06/article-06-04.asp>.

Center for Summer Learning. "Doesn't Every Child Deserve a Memorable Summer?" Feb. 2008. 19 Apr. 2008 <http://www.summerlearning.org/media/researchandpublications/Memorable.Summer.Fact.Sheet.Final.2.26.08.pdf>.

Center for Summer Learning. "Summertime and Weight Gain." 2007. 20 Apr. 2008 <http://www.summerlearning.org/media/researchandpublications/Summer.Weightgain.Brief.Final.pdf>.

Chesapeake Institute. "Attention Deficit Disorder: What Teachers Should Know." Undated. 21 Aug. 2008 <http://user.cybrzn.com/kenyonck/add/doe_tch.htm>.

Chicago Public Schools. "Small Schools Get Results." 2003. 19 Aug. 2007 <http://smallschools.cps.k12.il.us/research.html>.

Child Development Institute. "About Dyslexia & Reading Problems." Undated. 23 Aug. 2008 <http://www.childdevelopmentinfo.com/learning/dyslexia.shtml>.

College Board. "Advanced Placement Report to the Nation." 2007. 29 July 2008 <http://www.collegeboard.com/prod_downloads/about/news_info/ap/2007/2007_ap-report-nation.pdf>.

College Board. "The 4th Annual AP Report to the Nation." 2008. 29 July 2008 <http://professionals.collegeboard.com/profdownload/ap-report-to-the-nation-2008.pdf>.

Cooper, Harris. "Summer Learning Loss: The Problem and Some Solutions." 2003. 22 Aug. 2008 <http://www.ldonline.org/article/8057?theme=print>.

Corbett, Christianne, Catherine Hill, and Andresse St. Rose. "Where the Girls Are: The Facts about Gender Equity in Education." 2008. 31 July 3008 <http://www.aauw.org/research/WhereGirlsAre.cfm>.

Cotton, Kathleen. "New Small Learning Communities: Findings from Recent Literature." 2001. 19 Aug. 2008 <http://www3.scasd.org/small_schools/nlsc.pdf>.

Cotton, Kathleen. "Schoolwide and Classroom Discipline." School Improvement Research Series, Close-Up #9. 2001. 26 July 2008 <http://www.nwrel.org/scped/sirs/5/cu9.html>.

Curtain, Helena. "Foreign Language Learning: An Early Start, ERIC Digest." 1990. 2 Aug. 2008 <http://www.ericdigests.org/pre-9218/start.htm>.

Danielson, Lana. "The Improvement of Student Writing: What Research Says." 2000. 16 Aug. 2007 <http://www.ncacasi.org/jsi/2000v1i1/improvement>.

Delisio, Ellen. "Organizing Staff Meetings Even *You* Want to Attend." 2008. 22 Apr. 2008 <http://www.educationworld.com/a_admin/admin/admin518.shtml>.

Diamond, Marian. "What Are the Determinants of Children's Academic Successes and Difficulties?" 1999. 28 Aug. 2008 <http://www.newhorizons.org/neuro/diamond_determinants.htm>.

Diaz, Miriam. "Learning Strategies in the Secondary Foreign Language Classroom: An Essential Curriculum Component for Beginning Students." 2004. 2 Aug. 2008 <www.wm.edu/education/599/04projects/Diaz.pdf>.

Dunham, Will. "Magically Delicious: Breakfast Keeps Teens Lean." 3 Mar. 2008. 3 July 2008 <http://www.reuters.com/article/healthNews/idUSN2945373220080303?feedType=RSS&feedName=healthNews>.

Dunne, Diane. "Teachers Learn from Looking Together at Student Work." 2000. 30 July 2008 <http://www.education-world.com/a_curr/curr246.html>.

DuPaul, George, and George White. "An ADHD Primer." *Principal Leadership Magazine* (Oct. 2004): 1+. 21 Aug. 2008 <http://www.nasponline.org/resources/principals/nassp_adhd.aspx>.

Education Commission of the States. "Citizenship Education Inclusion in Assessment and Accountability

Systems." 2008. 24 Mar. 2008 <http://mb2.ecs.org/reports/Report.aspx?id=107>.

The Education Trust. "Effects of Student Achievement by Teachers in SIP Teams." 2007. 30 July 2008 <http://www2.edtrust.org/EdTrust/SIP+Professional+Development/Standards+in+practice+2.htm>.

Education World. "Great Meetings." Undated. 22 Apr. 2008 <http://www.education-world.com/a_admin/archives/greatmeetings.shtml>.

Evaluation Services Section, Public Schools of North Carolina. "Year-Round Schools and Achievement in North Carolina." 2000. 21 Aug. 2008 <http://www.ncpublicschools.org/docs/accountability/evaluation/evalbriefs/vol2n2-yr.pdf>.

Evans, Robert. "A Comparative Study of Student Achievement between Traditional Calendar Schools and Year-Round Schools in Indiana." 2007. 22 Aug. 2008 <http://docs.lib.purdue.edu/dissertations/AAI3287265/>.

Fiske, Edward B. *Learning in Deed: A Report from the National Commission on Service Learning*. Undated. 30 June 2008 <http://www.learningindeed.org/slcommission/learningindeed.pdf>.

Forsbach-Rothman, Terry, Marcia Margolin, and Diane Bloom. "Student Teachers and Alternate Route Teachers' Sense of Efficacy and Views of Teacher Preparation." 2007. 28 July 2008 <http://www.altteachercert.org/NAAC_Online_Journal_Spring_07_Issue.pdf>.

Franklin, Cheryl, and Mary Holm. "Looping—How Widespread Is Its Use? Rationale, Evidence Supporting Its Use." Undated. 18 Aug. 2008 <http://education.stateuniversity.com/pages/2194/Looping.html>.

Furman, Robert, and Richard Zibrida. "The Hurried Principal." 1990. 02 June 2008 <http://eric.ed.gov/ERICDocs/data/ericdocs2sql/content_storage_01/0000019b/80/13/45/7e.pdf>.

Gahala, Jan. "Critical Issue: Promoting Technology Use in Schools." 2001. 16 June 2008 <http://www.ncrel.org/sdrs/areas/issues/methods/technlgy/te200.htm>.

Glencoe. "Differentiating Instruction: Meeting Students Where They Are." Undated. 24 Mar. 2008 <http://www.glencoe.com/sec/teachingtoday/subject/di_meeting.phtml>.

Goldring, Ellen, Andrew Porter, Joseph Murphy, Stephen Elliott, and Xiu Cravens. "Assessing Learning-Centered Leadership." 2007. 24 July 2008 <http://www.wallacefoundation.org/NR/rdonlyres/2D4629AE-6592-4FDD-9206-D23A2B19EAC5/0/AssessingLearningCenteredLeadership.pdf>.

Goodman, Richard, and William Zimmerman. "Thinking Differently: Recommendations for 21st Century School Board/Superintendent Leadership, Governance, and Teamwork for High Student Achievement." 2000. 24 Mar. 2008 <http://www.nesdec.org/Thinking_Differently.htm>.

Gould, Holly. "Can Novice Teachers Differentiate Instruction? Yes, They CAN!" 2004. 24 Mar. 2008 <http://newhorizons.org/strategies/differentiated/gould.htm>.

Gulek, James, and Hakan Demirtas. "Learning with Technology: The Impact of Laptop Use on Student Achievement." *Journal of Technology, Learning, and Assessment* (Jan. 2005). 03 Mar. 2008 <http://escholarship.bc.edu/cgi/viewcontent.cgi?article=1052&context=jtla>.

Hall, Tracey. "Differentiated Instruction." Undated. 24 Mar. 2008 <http://www.cast.org/publications/ncac/ncac_diffinstructudl.html>.

Hallinger, Phillip. "Research on the Practice of Instructional and Transformational Leadership: Retrospect and Prospect." 2007. 24 July 2008 <http://www.acer.edu.au/documents/RC2007_Hallinger-RetrospectAndProspect.pdf>.

Hargrove, Thomas, and Guido Stempel. "Americans Wistful for Foreign Language in High School." 20 June 2007. 2 Aug. 2008 <http://newspolls.org/story.php?story_id=65>.

Hopkins, Gary. "Principals Offer Practical, Timely 'Time Management' Tips." Jan. 2006. 02 June 2008 <http://www.educationworld.com/a_admin/admin/admin436_a.shtm>l.

Huntley, Lance, and Tracy Greever-Rice. "Analysis of 2005 MAP Results for eMINTS Students." 2007. 03 Mar. 2008 <http://www.emints.org/evaluation/reports/map2005.pdf>.

International Dyslexia Association. "Dyslexia Basics." 2008. 23 Aug. 2008 <http://www.interdys.org/ewebeditpro5/upload/Basics_Fact_Sheet_5-08-08.pdf>.

Iowa Association of School Boards. "School Boards and Student Achievement." 2000. 24 Mar. 2008 <http://www.baraboo.k12.wi.us/schoolboard/compass_article.pdf>.

i-SAFE America Inc. "Beware of the Cyber Bully." Undated. 25 July 2008 <http://www.isafe.org/imgs/pdf/education/CyberBullying.pdf>.

Johnson, Deborah. "Critical Issue: Beyond Social Promotion and Retention—Five Strategies to Help Students Succeed." 2001. 12 Aug. 2008 <http://www.ncrel.org/sdrs/areas/issues/students/atrisk/at800.htm>.

Kaplan, Julie, and Diane Tracey. "Teacher Read-Alouds at 2nd Grade, with and without Student Companion Texts: Unexpected Findings." 2007. 9 July 2008 <http://eric.ed.gov/ERICDocs/data/ericdocs2sql/content_storage_01/0000019b/80/3d/e0/8a.pdf>.

Kittock, Janice, and Ryan Wertz. "World Language Graduation Requirements." 2008. 1 Aug. 2008 <http://www.ncssfl.org/reports2/States%20with%20Foreign%20Language%20Requirements.doc>.

Klump, Jennifer. "What the Research Says (or Doesn't Say) about K-8 Versus Middle School Grade Configurations." 2006. 24 Aug. 2008 <http://www.nwrel.org/nwedu/11-03/research/>.

Laine, Jaynae, and Debbie Hickst. "Common Threads Found among Schools Closing Achievement Gaps." 2008. 25 July 2008 <http://www.kltprc.net/foresight/Chpt_97_htm>.

Lance, Keith Curry, Marcia Rodney, Christine Hamilton-Pennell. "Powerful Libraries Make Powerful Learners: The Illinois Study." 2005. 26 Aug. 2008 <http://www.islma.org/pdf/ILStudy2.pdf>.

Lance, Keith Curry, Marcia Rodney, and Becky Russell. "How Students, Teachers, and Principals Benefit from Strong School Libraries: The Indiana Study—2007." 2007. 26 Aug. 2008 <http://www.ilfonline.org/AIME/ExecutiveSummary.pdf>.

Lashway, Larry. "Using School Board Policy to Improve Student Achievement." *ERIC Digest*. Undated. 24 Mar. 2008 <http://www.ericdigests.org/2003-4/school-board.html>.

Lauer, Patricia, et al. "The Effectiveness of Out-of-School-Time Strategies in Assisting Low-Achieving Students in Reading and Mathematics." 2003. 31 July 2008 <http://www.mcrel.org/PDF/SchoolImprovementReform/5032RR_RSOSTeffectiveness.pdf>.

Leithwood, Kenneth, Karen Louis, Stephen Anderson, and Kyla Wahlstrom. "How Leadership Influences Student Learning." 2004. 03 June 2008 <http://www.wallacefoundation.org/NR/rdonlyres/E3BCCFA5-A88B-45D3-8E27-B973732283C9/0/ReviewofResearchLearningFromLeadership.pdf>.

Lemke, Cheryl. "Why Does Technology Work in Some Schools and Not Others?" Undated. 07 Mar. 2008 <http://www.techlearning.com/techlearning/pdf/events/techforum/sd06/CherylKeynoteHandout.pdf>.

Looking at Student Work. "Protocols." Undated. 30 July 2008 <http://www.lasw.org/protocols.html>.

Mael, Fred, et. al. "Single-Sex Versus Coeducational Schooling: A Systematic Review." 2005. 31 July 2008 <http://www.ed.gov/rschstat/eval/other/single-sex/single-sex.pdf>.

Magnuson, Peter. "Finding Time." *Communicator* (Mar. 2003): 1+. 02 June 2008 <http://www.naesp.org/ContentLoad.do?contentId=197>.

McCloskey, Wendy, et. al. "Teacher Effectiveness, Student Achievement, & National Board Certified Teachers." June 2005. 29 July 2008 <http://www.nbpts.org/UserFiles/File/Teacher_Effectiveness_Student_Achievement_and_National_Board_Certified_Teachers_D_-_McColskey.pdf>.

McEntire, Nancy. "Grade Configuration in K-12 Schools." 2005. 24 Aug. 2008 <http://ceep.crc.uiuc.edu/poptopics/gradeconfig.html>.

McLaughlin, Barry. "Myths and Misconceptions about Second Language Learning." 1992. 2 Aug. 2008 <http://www.ncela.gwu.edu/pubs/ncrcdsll/epr5.htm>.

McPeake, Jacqueline. "The Principalship: A Study of the Principal's Time on Task from 1960 to the Twenty-First Century." 2006. 02 June 2008 <http://www.marshall.edu/etd/doctors/mcpeake-jaqueline-2007-phd.pdf>.

MedicineNet, Inc. "Dyslexia." 2002. 23 Aug. 2008 <http://www.medicinenet.com/dyslexia/article.htm>.

Miller, Beth. "The Learning Season: The Untapped Power of Summer to Advance Student Achievement." 2007. 22 Aug. 2008 <http://www.nmefdn.org/uploads/Learning_Season_ES.pdf>.

National Association for Sport and Physical Education. "Shape of the Nation Report." 2006. 2 July 2008 <http://www.americanheart.org/downloadable/heart/1154607764279ShapeOfTheNation.pdf>.

National Association for Year-Round Education. "Statistical Summaries of Year-Round Education Programs: 2006-2007." Undated. 21 Aug. 2008 <http://www.nayre.org/STATISTICAL%20SUMMARIES%20OF%20YRE%202007.pdf>.

National Association of School Psychologists. "Position Statement on Student Grade Retention and Social Promotion." 2003. 12 Aug. 2008 <http://www.nasponline.org/about_nasp/pospaper_graderetent.aspx>.

National Association of State Directors of Special Education. "Myths about Response to Intervention." 2006. 24 Mar. 2008 <http://www.nasdse.org/documents/Myths%20about%20RtI.pdf>.

National Board for Professional Teaching Standards. "National Board Certification Statistics." 2007. 29 July 2008 <http://www.nbpts.org/about_us/2007_national_board_cert1/national_board_certifica/>.

National Center for Chronic Disease Prevention and Health Promotion. "Coordinated School Health Program." 2007. 2 July 2008 <http://www.cdc.gov/HealthyYouth/CSHP/>.

National Center for Education Statistics. "Fast Facts." 2008. 18 Aug. 2008 <http://nces.ed.gov/fastfacts/display.asp?id=4>.

National Center for Education Statistics. "The Nation's Report Card: Civics 2006." 2007. 25 Mar. 2008 <http://nces.ed.gov/nationsreportcard/civics/>.

National Center for Education Statistics. "The Nation's Report Card: Economics 2006." 2007. 25 Mar. 2008 <http://nces.ed.gov/nationsreportcard/economics/>.

National Center for Education Statistics. "The Nation's Report Card: Geography 2001." 2002. 25 Mar. 2008 <http://nces.ed.gov/nationsreportcard/geography/>.

National Center for Education Statistics. "The Nation's Report Card: U.S. History 2006." 2007. 25 Mar. 2008 <http://nces.ed.gov/nationsreportcard/ushistory/>.

National Center for Education Statistics. "The Nation's Report Card: Writing." 2008. 30 Aug. 2008 <http://nces.ed.gov/nationsreportcard/writing/>.

The National Commission on Writing. "Writing: A Ticket to Work . . . Or a Ticket Out." The College Board. 2006. 8 June 2008 <http://www.writingcommission.org/prod_downloads/writingcom/writing-ticket-to-work.pdf>.

The National Commission on Writing, "Writing and School Reform." The College Board. 2006. 24 Mar. 2008 <http://www.writingcommission.org/prod_downloads/writingcom/writing-school-reform-natl-comm-writing.pdf>.

National Council of Teachers of English. "What Research Says about Writing." Undated. 8 June 2008 <http://www.ncte.org/prog/writing/research>.

National Institute of Mental Health. *Autism Spectrum Disorders (Pervasive Developmental Disorders)*. 2007. 18 Aug. 2008 <http://www.nimh.nih.gov/health/publications/autism/nimhautismspectrum.pdf>

National School Boards Association. "Key Work of School Boards." Undated. 24 Mar. 2008 <http://www.nsba.org/MainMenu/Governance/KeyWork/Resources/KeyWorkComponentDescriptions/TeamLeadershipRolesampResponsibilities.aspx>.

National Youth Leadership Council. "Growing to Greatness 2007: The State of Service Learning." 2007. 1 July 2008 <http://www.nylc.org/inaction_init.cfm?oid=3698>.

National Youth Leadership Council. "Growing to Greatness 2008: The State of Service Learning." 2008. 1 July 2008 <http://www.nylc.org/objects/publications/8030548_Body.pdf>.

New York State Education Department. "New York Statewide Summer Reading Program 2008. Research/Promoting Literacy." Apr. 2008. 19 Apr. 2008 <http://www.sharingsuccess.org/code/bv/summerschool.pdf>.

North Central Regional Educational Laboratory. "Critical Issue: Using Technology to Improve Student Achievement." 2005. 16 June 2008 <http://www.ncrel.org/sdrs/areas/issues/methods/technlgy/te800.htm>.

O'Brien, Eileen. "Making Time: What Research Says about Reorganizing School Schedules." 2006. 22 Aug. 2008 <http://www.centerforpubliceducation.org/site/c.kjJXJ5MPIwE/b.2086551/k.9967/Making_time>.

The Ontario Library Association. "School Libraries and Student Achievement in Ontario." 2006. 26 Aug. 2008 <http://www.accessola.com/data/6/rec_docs/137_eqao_pfe_study_2006.pdf>.

Osborne, Cliff. "BETTER Social Studies: Building Effective Teaching through Educational Research." Undated. 30 July 2008 <http://eric.ed.gov/ERICDocs/data/ericdocs2sql/content_storage_01/0000019b/80/13/b9/9f.pdf>.

Parsad, Basmat, and Laurie Lewis. "Remedial Education at Degree-Granting Postsecondary Institutions in Fall 2000." *Education Statistics Quarterly* (Aug. 2004). 8 June 2008 <http://nces.ed.gov/programs/quarterly/vol_5/5_4/4_4.asp#2>.

Pennsylvania Office of Attorney General. "Cyber Bullying." Undated. 25 July 2008 <http://www.attorneygeneral.gov/kidsparents.aspx?id=1567>.

President's Commission on Special Education. "A New Era: Revitalizing Special Education for Children and Their Families." 2002. 24 Mar. 2008 <http://www.ed.gov/inits/commissionsboards/whspecialeducation/reports/images/Pres_Rep.pdf>.

The Principals' Partnership. "Research Brief: More on Block Schedules." Undated. 12 Aug. 2008 <http://www.principalspartnership.com/blockschedules2.pdf>.

Reuters Health. "Teens, Parents May Not See a Weight Problem." 2008. 2 July 2008 <http://www.reuters.com/article/healthNews/idUSKIM95354620080219>.

Richardson, Joan. "Harness the Potential of Staff Meetings." Oct. 1999. 30 July 2008 <http://www.nsdc.org/library/publications/tools/tools10-99rich.cfm>.

RMC Research Corporation. "Impacts of Service-Learning on Participating K-12 Students. (Expanded)" 2007. 1 July 2008 <http://www.servicelearning.org/instant_info/fact_sheets/k-12_facts/impacts/expanded.php>.

Rudy, Lisa Jo. *Your Guide to Autism*. 2007. 17 Nov. 2007 <http://autism.about.com>.

Salahu-Din, Debra, Hilary Persky, and Jessica Miller. "The Nation's Report Card: Writing 2007." 2008. 8 June 2008 <http://nces.ed.gov/pubsearch/pubsinfo.asp?pubid=2008468>.

Salvetti, Elizabeth. "Looping: Supporting Student Learning through Long-Term Relationships." 1997. 18 Aug. 2008 <http://www.alliance.brown.edu/pubs/ic/looping/looping.pdf>.

Sanders, William, James Ashton, and Paul Wright. "Comparison of the Effects of NBPTS Certified Teachers with Other Teachers on the Rates of Student Academic Progress." Mar., 2006. 29 July 2008 <http://www.nbpts.org/UserFiles/File/SAS_final_NBPTS_report_D_-_Sanders.pdf>.

Sawyer, Gayle, and Belinda Gimbert. "Policies and Practices for Selecting Highly Effective Teachers for Alternative Certification Programs." 2008. 30 July 2008 <http://www.alt-teachercert.org/NAAC_Online_Journal_Spring_08_Issue.pdf>.

Scott, Mary. "Attention Deficit Disorder (ADD). Digest #445." 1987. 21 Aug. 2008 <http://www.ericdigests.org/pre-927/add.htm>.

Southern Regional Education Board. "Summer School: Unfulfilled Promise." 2002. 19 Apr. 2008 <http://www.sreb.org/programs/srr/pubs/Summer_School.pdf>.

Starzyk, Edith, and Scott Stephens. "More Often, Path to Classroom Is an Indirect Route." 2008. 30 July 2008 <http://www.innovations.harvard.edu/news/100391.html>.

Thompson, Charles, and Elizabeth Cunningham. "Retention and Social Promotion: Research and Implications for Policy. ERIC Digest Number 161." 2000. 12 Aug. 2008 <http://www.ericdigests.org/2001-3/policy.htm>.

Todd, Ross. "Student Learning through Ohio School Libraries." 2003. 26 Aug. 2008 <http://www.oelma.org/StudentLearning/documents/OELMAResearchStudy8page.pdf>.

Trelease, Jim. "Chapter 1: Why Read Aloud?" *The Read-Aloud Handbook*. 2001. 8 July 2008 <http//:www.trelease-on-reading.com/rah_chpt1_p2.html>.

Trelease, Jim. "Chapter 5: Sustained Silent Reading—Reading Aloud's Natural Partner." *The Read-Aloud Handbook*. 2001. 8 July 2008 <http//:www.trelease-on-reading.com/rah_chpt5_p1.html>.

Tucker, Bill. "Laboratories of Reform: Virtual High Schools and Innovation in Public Education." 2007. 19 June 2008 <http://www.educationsector.org/usr_doc/Virtual_Schools.pdf>.

UCLA School Mental Health Project. "Summer and the Living Ain't Easy." June 2003. 19 Apr. 2008 <http://smhp.psych.ucla.edu/atyourschool/june03.htm>.

United States Department of Education. "Prisoners of Time." 1994. 21 Aug. 2008 <http://www.ed.gov/pubs/PrisonersOfTime/Prisoners.html>.

United States Department of Education. "Implementation Study of Smaller Learning Communities: Final Report." 2008. 19 Aug. 2008 <http://www.ed.gov/rschstat/eval/other/small-communities/highlights.doc>.

University of Kansas. "An Introduction to Writing." *Special Connections*. Undated. 8 June 2008 <http://www.specialconnections.ku.edu/cgi-bin/cgiwrap/specconn/main.php?cat=instruction&section=main&subsection=writing/main>.

von Zastrow, Claus. *Academic Atrophy: The Condition of the Liberal Arts in America's Public Schools.* 2004. 24 Mar. 2008 <http://www.music-for-all.org/documents/cbe_principal_Report.pdf>.

Waits, Mary Jo. "Why Some Schools with Latino Children BEAT THE ODDS . . . and Others Don't." 2006. 30 July 2008 <http://www.arizonafuture.org/latinoEd/FAZ502_LatinEd_final.pdf>.

Walker, Karen. "Research Brief: 7-12 Grade Configuration." 2005. 24 Aug. 2008 <http://www.principalspartnership.com/712configuration.pdf>.

Walker, Karen. "Research Brief: Summer School." 2004. 19 Apr. 2008 <http://www.principalspartnership.com/summerschool.pdf>.

Watson, John, and Jennifer Ryan. "Keeping Pace with K-12 Online Learning." 2006. 19 June 2008 <http://www.nacol.org/docs/Keeping%20Pace%20with%20K-12%20Online%20Learning%202006.pdf>.

Waxman, Hersh, Meng-Fen Lin, and Georgette Michko. "A Meta-Analysis of the Effectiveness of Teaching and Learning with Technology on Student Outcomes." 2003. 03Mar. 2008 <http://www.ncrel.org/tech/effects2/waxman.pdf>.

West Regional Equity Network. "About Cyber-Bullying." 2008. 25 July 2008 <http://www.ed.arizona.edu/wren/bully_cyber_about.html.>

Wootan, Margo. "State School Foods Report Card 2007." 2007. 2 July 2008 <http://www.cspinet.org/2007schoolreport.pdf>.

Wynne, Joan. "Teachers as Leaders in Education Reform." Undated. 25 June 2008 <http://www.ericdigests.org/2002-4/teachers.html>.

Xu, Zeyu, Jane Hannaway, and Colin Taylor. "Making a Difference?" The Effects of Teach for America in High School." 2007. 30 July 2008 <http://www.urban.org/UploadedPDF/411642_Teach_America.pdf>.

Yakimowski, Mary, and Faith Connolly. "An Examination of K-5, 6-8 Versus K-8 Grade Configurations." 2001 24 Aug. 2008 <http://www.bcps.k12.md.us/Student_Performance/PDF/IR_K5_6_8_Comprehensive_Report_Nov2001.pdf>.

INDEX

Abecedarian Project 30
access
    books 50, 51
    computers 58-60
    course 76, 77
    healthy meals 53
    liberal arts 111
accommodations 21
achievement 2, 3, 6-8, 26, 32, 37-45, 48-52, 54, 55, 60, 61, 63, 71, 74, 80, 82, 92-94, 96, 98, 102, 106, 110, 114, 115, 120
achievement gap 8, 26, 50-52, 96, 110, 114
achievement loss 50
ACT 94, 107
administrative presence 15
Advanced Placement 38, 74-77
African-American 48, 76, 77, 82, 86, 96, 110
alignment 3, 12, 59, 115
American Association of School Administrators 55
American Council of Teachers of Foreign Languages 93
American Psychological Association 24
Arizona Geographic Alliance 113
articulation 93
assessment 2, 3, 5, 12, 18-20, 27, 29, 31, 37, 39, 40, 42, 48, 49, 54, 58-60, 69, 82, 86, 96, 97, 100, 106, 110, 111
attendance 33, 36, 42, 48, 114
attention 6, 20, 21, 24, 25, 31, 39, 43, 49, 58, 66, 67, 70, 75, 77, 92, 97, 98, 102, 104, 105, 107, 121
attention deficit/hyperactivity disorder 24, 25, 32
autism 20, 21

background knowledge 27, 70, 104, 113
barriers 43, 55, 59, 100
Becoming a Nation of Readers 102
behavior 10, 12, 20, 25, 48, 56, 112, 115, 118, 119
    disruptive 20, 120, 122, 123
    repetitive 20
board of education 2, 3, 118
body mass index 53, 86
book studies 12
brain 22, 32, 33, 66-71
Bright Solutions 22
bullies, cyber 118, 119

Caine, Renate and Geoffrey 70
Center for Science in the Public Interest 88
central office 5, 55
certification
    alternative 80, 81
    national board 82, 83
Chesapeake Institute 24
Chicago Child-Parent Centers 30
Child Development Institute 22
choices 53, 67, 101
chunking 68, 69
class size 6, 27, 30, 52, 80, 106
classroom management 120-123
climate (school) 6, 39, 45, 70, 112, 120
cognitive ability 92
collaboration 13, 26, 43, 60, 74, 93, 107, 115
College Board 74, 76, 77, 100
college performance 74
Collins, Jim 26
Commission on Reading 102, 104
communication 3, 15, 19, 20, 63, 95, 118, 119, 122
community 7, 37, 43, 54, 114, 115
context 4, 6, 10, 67-70, 95
Council for Basic Education 111
Council of Chief State School Officers 36
counseling 23, 63,95
culture
    of language 26, 95, 112,113
    school 5-7, 9, 11
curriculum 4, 5, 9, 12, 14, 18, 19, 27-29, 31, 45, 52, 58, 75, 87, 92, 93, 100, 101, 107, 111

data 4-6, 10-12, 14, 15, 18, 26-29, 31, 36, 38-42, 45, 49-52, 54, 58, 62, 75, 76, 80, 86, 94, 96, 100, 114, 118
data management 58
DataWorks 12
decision-making 28
delegation 15
differentiation 18, 19, 26, 28, 33, 71, 98, 121
discipline 32, 33, 39, 55, 120, 122, 123
distance learning 62
dropouts 26, 32, 48, 50, 51, 114
dyslexia 22, 23, 32
early childhood 30, 31

Education Commission of the States 110
efficacy 54, 70, 80, 81, 115
Elementary and Secondary Education Act 60
emotion 66, 68-71
English language learners 26, 27, 44, 54, 93, 94, 112, 113
enrichment 52, 71
environment 7, 12, 19, 32, 39, 42, 44, 54, 69-71, 103
exercise 87, 88
expectations 2-7, 14, 25-27, 29, 43, 48, 54, 55, 74, 87, 98, 99, 102, 110, 122
extracurricular activities 41, 42

families (see parents)
feedback 71, 98
Florida Virtual High School 62, 63
food services 88

gender 20, 24, 32, 33, 45
gender gap 32
goals 39, 55, 60, 71, 88, 93, 115
grade point average (GPA) 52, 74, 75, 114
grade retention 30, 32, 48, 49
grade-level configuration 40, 41
graduation rate 30, 33, 42
graphic organizers 69
grouping 6, 18, 48

hardware 58-60
High/Scope Perry Preschool 30
Hispanic students 26, 27, 48, 76, 77, 82, 86, 96, 110
homework 19

impulsiveness 24
inattention 24
individual differences 70
Individuals with Disabilities Act 28
instructional practices 6, 18, 19, 22, 23, 25-29, 33, 52, 53, 59, 60, 66, 68-70, 81, 83, 92, 93, 95, 98, 99, 100-102, 104, 107, 112, 113, 120, 121
interaction 8, 10, 12, 20, 21, 39, 41, 52, 60, 67, 69, 70, 95, 105, 113
International Dyslexia Association 22
international language
    elementary level 92, 93
    secondary level 92, 94, 95
Internet 58, 118, 119
Interstate School Leaders Licensure Consortium 7
interventions 23, 25, 26, 28, 29, 32, 41, 45, 49, 52, 53
Iowa Association of School Board 2
i-Safe 118, 119

junk foods 89

kindergarten 12, 20, 48, 49, 51, 66
Krashen, Steven 102

leadership 2-9, 15, 27, 83
learning (see achievement)
learning disability 28
learning strategies 95
least restrictive environment 21
librarians 106, 107
libraries 50, 51, 106, 107
Looking at Student Work 12, 13
looping 44, 45
low income (see socioeconomic status)

Marzano, Robert 121, 122

Index / 131

mathematics computation 50
media specialists (see librarians)
memory 68-70, 95
Mid-continent Research for Education and Learning 6, 54
mission 6, 43, 54
mobility 45, 48
monitor
    instruction 4
    programs and practices 6, 7
    student progress 2, 6, 29, 120, 121
    use of time 39
Morrison Institute for Public Policy 26
motivation 70, 104, 114
multiple-track schools 36

Nation at Risk, A 6, 36
National Assessment Governing Board 110
National Assessment of Educational Progress 22, 60, 96, 100, 110
National Association of State Directors of Special Education 28
National Board of Professional Teaching Standards 82
National Board-certified Teachers 8, 82, 83
National Center for Chronic Disease Prevention and Health Promotion 87, 88
National Center for Education Statistics 30
National Clearinghouse for English Language Acquisition 112
National Commission on Service Learning 114
National Commission on Time and Learning 36
National Commission on Writing 100
National Council of Teachers of English 99
National Institute of Health 22
National Reading Panel 102
National School Boards Association 3
National Youth Leadership Council 114, 115
ninth graders 40, 42, 48
No Child Left Behind 38, 80, 92, 94, 97, 110, 114
norms 10, 12
note taking 25
novelty 66, 67
nutrition 52, 71, 88, 89

obesity 52, 86-89
online learning (see virtual learning)
overweight 52, 86, 87

parents 15, 19, 21, 24, 27, 31, 43-45
patterns 70
phonemic awareness 22, 23, 28
phonics 22, 23, 28
physical activity 25, 53, 69, 71, 86, 87, 95
physical education 86-88

planning 15, 16, 43, 53, 55, 59, 69, 71, 81, 83, 94, 98, 102, 107, 115, 120, 121, 123
plans
    school improvement 4, 5, 88
    strategic 4
policies 2, 3, 7, 9, 48, 57, 62, 76, 81, 88, 99, 101, 119
prerequisite knowledge 61
preschool 24, 30, 31, 49, 51, 104, 105
principal 5-15, 26, 27, 55, 107, 120
prior knowledge (see background knowledge)
priorities 14, 15, 58
Prisoners of Time 36
processing time 68, 69
professional development 2-5, 8-10, 12, 13, 19, 21, 25, 29, 31, 33, 39, 41, 43, 45, 58, 59, 61, 77, 99, 101, 111
program evaluation 31, 39, 45, 53, 59, 63, 101, 103, 115
protocols 10, 12, 29
proximity 123

RAND Corporation 54
Read-Aloud Handbook, The 104
reading 22, 23, 25, 27, 28, 31, 50-52, 54, 99, 100
    aloud 104, 105
    comprehension 28, 47, 50, 51, 104
    fluency 28, 102
    independent 102, 105
    loss 50
    sustained silent 102, 103
relevance 13, 53, 66
remediation 49, 52, 53, 61
Response to Intervention (RTI) 23, 28, 29, 49
routines 21, 24, 44, 67, 98, 104
rules 23, 24, 122, 123
rural schools 40, 58

SAT 74, 75, 94
safe environment 7, 12
scheduling
    block 38, 39
    flexible 106
school improvement goals 2, 13
school size 42, 43
senses 23, 70
service learning 114, 115
single-grade centers 40
single-sex education 32, 33
site-based management 4
skills
    critical thinking 112
    higher-order thinking 61
    research 60, 61
    social 24
sleep 66, 69
small learning communities 42, 43
social promotion 48, 49
social studies 92, 110-113

socioeconomic status 30, 37, 40, 50-52, 54, 58, 61, 75, 77, 93, 106, 114
software 59-61
special education 22, 28-30, 32, 39
spelling 22, 23, 50, 98
staff development (see professional development)
staff meetings 10-13
standards
    academic 3, 12, 97, 112, 114
    nutrition 88
summer learning loss 36, 37
summer programs 52, 53
summer slide 50, 51
superintendent 2-5, 14, 55
support for learning 7

Teach for America 81
teachers
    as leaders 8, 9, 82, 83
    assignment 81
    beginning 19, 81
    mentoring 8, 9, 31, 71
    quality 30, 31, 52, 80-83, 92, 120, 121
technology 58-63, 96, 97, 99, 118, 119
    computers 58-60, 96, 106
    digital whiteboards 58
    laptops 60
    streaming video 58, 59
thematic instruction 68
Third International Math and Science Study 75
time 3, 6-8, 10-15, 18, 19, 21, 25, 36-39, 43, 44, 52, 54, 59, 60, 62, 63, 66-70, 81, 86, 87, 93, 95-97, 99, 100, 102-105, 107, 111-113, 121
Title IX 32
transitions 25, 41, 48, 49, 121
Trelease, Jim 104
tutoring 21, 54, 60

United States Department of Agriculture 88
United States Department of Education 44, 70, 122
urban schools 4, 12, 45

vertical articulation 75, 77
virtual learning 62, 63
vision 3, 6, 7, 43, 59
visualization 68
vocabulary 27, 28, 30, 45, 50, 92, 93, 95, 98, 100, 102, 104, 105, 112, 113

walkthroughs, instructional 5
West Regional Equity Network 118
with-it-ness 120, 121, 123
writing 18, 33, 45, 60, 92, 95-101

year-round schools 36, 37